MINDFULNESS
FOR THE MINDLESS

A NO NONESENSE GUIDE TO BREAKING FREE FROM A MINDLESS LIFE

JOHN BURLEY

MINDFULNESS
FOR THE MINDLESS

This edition first published in 2018.

Copyright © 2018 John Burley

A catalogue record for this book is available from the British Library.

Fonts:
Oswald by Vernon Adams
EB Garamond by George Duffner

ISBN: 978-1-9999953-0-0

DISCLAIMER

This book is for informational purposes only and the author, his agents, heirs, and assignees do not accept any responsibilities for any liabilities, actual or alleged, resulting from the use of this information.

This book is not "professional advice". The author encourages the reader to seek advice from a professional where any reasonably prudent person would do so. While every reasonable attempt has been made to verify the information contained in this book, the author and his affiliates cannot assume any responsibility for errors, inaccuracies or omissions, including omissions in transmission or reproduction.

Any reference to people, events, organisations, or business entities are for educational and illustrative purposes only, and no intent to falsely characterise, recommend, disparage, or injure is intended or should be so construed. Any results stated or implied are consistent with general results, but this means results can and will vary. The author, his agents, and assigns, make no promises or guarantees, stated or implied. Individual results will vary and this work is supplied strictly on an "at your own risk" basis.

10% of all author royalties from this book are donated to Mind: For better mental health.

Mind is a UK based charity (219830) providing advice and support to empower anyone experiencing a mental health problem. They campaign to improve services, raise awareness and promote understanding.

Every year, one in four of us will experience a mental health problem. Yet hundreds of thousands of people are still struggling. Mind believe that no-one should have to face a mental health problem alone. They will listen, give you support and advice, and fight your corner.

For immediate help with mental health issues visit www.mind.org.uk, call 0300 123 3393 or text 86463.

Mind is not affiliated or associated with this book or its contents in anyway. Mind has not read or endorsed this book.

To Megan,
who inspired the journey of a lifetime.

To Jenny,
who has shown me the way more than once.

CONTENTS

INTRODUCTION

Mindless

Adjective | Mind - less

1.   lack of consciousness or mind
2.   not mindful

I live in a bright and colourful world full of interesting people, different cultures, amazing animals and a wonderfully diverse nature. A world that makes every moment worth savouring and enjoying as much as possible. I awake each morning not knowing what the world has to offer me today differently to yesterday. Sounds good doesn't it? Well you live in a world very similar to mine.

After I'd started actively practising mindfulness I noticed some immediate benefits, for example, strangers smiling at me in the street, my general outlook was a bit more positive and I was more inclined to see my own and others mistakes as opportunities to learn. My friends and family immediately noticed the difference and started to ask what had changed in my life to cause a such a dramatic change. The quality and speed of my work improved almost overnight. Customers and people that I worked alongside also noticed a difference in my approach too.

Once I'd explained it was down to me practising mindfulness they all wanted to try it and realise the same change as I'd had. While I could point them to my reading list on mindfulness, I quickly realised that there wasn't just one book that gave them enough information and guidance to start seeing the benefits as quickly as most of them would like.

As with most people, before I'd started practising mindfulness I'd heard and seen many books in the shops about it. From the very little that I had heard about mindfulness in the media and from what I'd heard from other people it all sounded a bit wishy washy and too woo woo for me, and I knew I certainly didn't have time to sit around all day meditating. I had been told that it would help and I should give it a go several times but I'd had no idea where to start and it wasn't clear what I was going to gain from doing it anyway.

There are what seem like thousands of books on mindfulness in the bookshops and online, all with their own takes and viewpoints on how to practice mindfulness and get various benefits from it. People who already practice mindfulness will suggest books to you and quote wonderful and sometimes truly inspiring sound bites from those books to make you think there is something great to be found in mindfulness. But they all suggest different books and who has the time to read them all just to find the one book that explains mindfulness in a way that works just for you?

What I did was listen to the people closest to me that had actually read books on mindfulness instead of those who just quoted what they thought they knew from the media and social media posts. They were the people that lived in my world and would likely have a similar outlook to me, so in theory they would have been looking for similar benefits to me from mindfulness. This was my logic but it still meant reading many books.

When you start reading these books there are some noticeable reoccurring problems that I found. Either the books were long and included everything possible about mindfulness, from the history of mindfulness to every possible benefit mindfulness could bring you if you dedicated vast amounts of time to it. After reading some of these you feel so overwhelmed with all the information that you're given that you become less mindful because you're now trying to think and digest it all. At the other end you have short books and e-books that get straight to point and tell you how to practice mindfulness and meditation techniques without explaining what you are trying to achieve with them. Some just talk in general terms without actually giving you useful instructions and some leave you feeling like you've wasted a few hours that you'll never get back.

I am not saying that any of these books are bad, in fact in almost every book that I have read I have found something useful to take away, make me think or just a better explanation of something I'd read in another book. I would also say that with the way, speed and focus that I read with, it is actually a good step towards being mindful in itself, as I shut out all the other chatter in my head so all this reading hasn't been all bad on a mindful front probably.

So here is another book on mindfulness! The intention of this book is to provide a quick way to understand the principles of being mindful, so you can see some of the benefits as quickly as possible in your everyday life without having to give too much of your time to it initially. Mindfulness can help in many different areas, but my focus will be on just getting you started and helping you to see some close to instant improvements in your life. I will try to explain how to do it and what you can expect to gain by doing it in the shortest way and yet still give you enough information so you understand how it works. I will combine all the best explanations and methods that I have found so far from all of my reading on mindfulness to save you having to trawl the book shops. Like I explained earlier, once I'd actually bitten the bullet and given it a go, I got results almost overnight.

Unlike many other books, I will not make you wade through chapters explaining the history and how to become some kind of mindfulness meditation master. This isn't what this book is about. Anyone can be mindful and feel the benefits to their general well-being, so you have no reason not give this a go, it's completely free and it certainly won't hurt you.

This is my first attempt at writing a book so please forgive any errors and while I find my style. Thank you for taking the time to read this book and I hope you start seeing the your world and life in a new and wonderful way.

1

MINDFULNESS

Mindfulness

Noun | Mind - ful – ness

1.   State or quality of being mindful
2.   The practice of a non-judgemental state
or awareness of one's feelings, emotions, thoughts and
experiences in the present

Mindfulness is just about deliberately paying attention to what is happening right now (the present moment) along with some curiosity, kindness and an accepting mentality.

Something to remember now you've started on your mindfulness journey is that if you become more mindful you will likely have better general well-being and become happier. Not only that, as you become happier, the people around you and those you interact with will also see the benefits and will likely be a bit happier too (especially when around you). And we all know that on the whole human beings prefer to be around happy people over unhappy people.

Mindfulness has been around for centuries and is found in ancient cultures from all parts of the world. Mindfulness translates from an ancient Buddhist term "Sati" which means awareness of things and their relationship to other things which provides an awareness of their value. How much value do you place on your time and experiences?

Practising mindfulness is about being in and experiencing the present moment, as this moment is the only time that is actually real. The past and the future only exist inside your head in either your memory or your imagination. So the only moment we all truly have is this moment right now. The present moment is the only time where you can live, make decisions, think, take actions and live your life. Mindfulness is all about understanding this and spending less time inside your head and much more time experiencing the present moment itself, which will in turn lead to a calmer, kinder and more fulfilled existence for yourself and others around you.

More Attentive

Being mindful is purely focusing and being attentive to what you are doing or experiencing right now. Life is happening continuously around us all the time, yet often we don't even notice because we aren't concentrating or paying attention to it. Yes, some of the present moments can be pretty boring and it's easy to drift off into your own memory or imagination but when you actually pay attention, even to the boring moments, there is often something there that you haven't noticed before that is interesting. It could be a sound, a smell or something you haven't seen before.

Even if while you are paying attention, you don't notice anything new, you are mindfully not noticing anything new because you are paying attention. The point is, you are here and experiencing real life in the present moment even if it happens to be a boring moment just now.

Studies have shown that drivers on average only take in one out of five road signs when driving on the roads. We all know what it's like to get to a destination and not be able to remember the journey we took in any real detail. This is especially the case for journeys that we make regularly, like the school run or to and from work. This is because we aren't really paying attention, we have other things going on inside our minds. Think about how much of your life you are missing if you are missing that many road signs!

Example: Just ask yourself "what am I paying attention to right now?". This involves taking a step back mentally and observing your own mind in action. You can then watch as your attention moves to something else. You will also notice a mental commentary going on inside your head too. Something like, "I'm focusing on this book" and "now I'm focusing on something I just heard and wondering what the hell it was". You are observing and paying attention to your own thoughts, as well as paying attention to something else - cool don't you think? This means you are self aware.

You can take this a step further and start turning your

attention to why your mind's attention is on that sound you heard instead of fully attentive to the words on this page. Once you start to pay attention you'll notice there is a lot more going on in your present life than you first realised.

And while you were paying attention to my little example your brain had a little rest from the usual background self talk too.

More Present

If you imagine that every moment equates to a second in time, how many do you have left in total? A lot I hope but it's about 7 or 8 less than when you started reading this paragraph already. See how quickly they are disappearing. How many are you missing the full experience of because your mind is consumed with something that happened this morning or might happen later today? How many have you not fully appreciated so far in your life?

Isn't about time you started being just a bit more present in these moments and enjoyed what life has to offer just a little bit more? Before you panic that time is running out for you, there are well over 31 million seconds each year so you have some time to get your head around all this but they are still ticking away as you read.

What you are doing now by trying to understand how to be more mindful will help you realise how to appreciate more of the present moments (seconds) so you'll actually gain some that you would had missed previously in the future if you hadn't turned to mindfulness.

It doesn't matter what is actually happening right now in the present moment, "it is what it is" as they say. Your experience is yours, totally valid and correct exactly as it is. It's just the way things are in this moment, but at least you actually know how they are right now because you're being present.

Example: Just stop reading at the end of this paragraph for 10 seconds and close your eyes. What sounds can you hear? Don't label them, just notice the sound itself and any others that you can hear. Don't think to yourself, that's an aeroplane overhead, someone cutting their grass down the street because you are now recalling things from memory which isn't part of being present. Notice any new sounds as they arrive at your ears or any that stop. Go on give it a go for 10 seconds.

There you go, give yourself a pat on the back, you were

just in the present for 10 seconds. I know it's hard to not give the sounds a label but even if you did label them you were still more present and more mindful than you would have been for the 10 seconds prior.

React Less

A reaction is something you do automatically when you experience something, usually due to past conditioning. When you react you are usually at a disadvantage as you have less or no control due to your lack of a considered response. Reactions tend to be emotionally driven, sporadic and often do not help any situation improve. Mindfully responding can have the opposite effect though.

We all know when someone is reacting to the emotion of a situation and not considering their responses. It is not uncommon for people on the other side of a disagreement to use the fact that you only react to their advantage. When you only react you can hand control of yourself to another person without realising.

The alternative is to mindfully respond instead of just blindly reacting without any thought. The urge to react is always there in many of us, but if you are mindful of the present you can catch the reaction, think and then only respond if a response is needed.

Even if you don't catch the reaction initially you will at least notice that you are reacting and quickly bring yourself back under control so you can respond more appropriately.

Mindfully responding may be more passive as it takes a bit more time to think and then come back with a more considered response, but it will lose you less friends in the long run. Remember, now that you're experiencing the present more, why not make it a happier, more enjoyable and less volatile present without thoughtless reactions.

Judge Less

We all have the temptation to judge any experience as either good or bad because we all like feeling happiness and none of us like feeling sadness. Often your judgements are more based upon past experiences and less on what you are actually experiencing in this moment. Judging holds us back and if we can judge less we can experience a richer, more meaningful and fulfilled life based around your true self.

It is possible to reduce and let go of judgements regardless of how repetitive or ingrained they are by using your new mindfulness skills. Your judgements are simply just thoughts in your mind and the choice is yours to how much value and credibility you give these thoughts.

When you pay attention to your thoughts, emotions, feelings and actions, you can identify the unhelpful thoughts and question whether they are true and valid for what is actually happening in the present.

It's not just about how we judge others, how we judge ourselves is far more important. Research has shown that our minds are telling ourselves stories continuously. These stories are about who we are, where we are going, what our relationship is to whoever we are with, etc. Albeit not necessarily true these stories are fine while they are all positive but what about when they become negative? What if we're telling ourself we are not good enough, we don't deserve something that makes you happy or successful.

Most of us have our own self doubts, but when they start to accumulate they start affecting our self esteem and sense of worth. It's very easy to incorrectly judge a situation and then make further judgements on the first incorrect assumption and so on. Before you know it you have spiralled miles away from the reality of the present basing incorrect assumption upon incorrect assumption. If you find you are doubting yourself, or having some negative thoughts just simply start to pay attention.

Paying attention to these thoughts will stop the internal storytelling automatically. Then ask yourself which of the thoughts I've just had do I know to be actually true. Think like you are giving evidence in a court and under oath, you wouldn't speculate and only say what you know for sure is true. Unless you can say one hundred percent that what you have been thinking is true you will discard it automatically.

Once you have done this, smile to yourself as you have just taken back control of your own thoughts, stopped a potential self judgement or negative thought pattern spiralling out of control and replaced it with a positive judgement of yourself. As you are now in control of your thoughts, you are definitely here in this moment.

Obviously you can apply the same logic to thoughts and judgements you are having about other people too as they all take place inside your mind.

More Compassion
True compassion isn't based upon attachments or desires. To show compassion is to understand and recognise that you have your own limitations and

flaws, as does everyone else and to forgive yourself and others for their mistakes, negative thoughts and fears.

We are all generally the same underneath with the same hopes and desires of being happy without any suffering. Understanding that if you peel away our exteriors, we are all essentially the same underneath, with the same desires and needs. Remembering this will help you to be more compassionate to others.

Be more compassionate to yourself, feelings of anger, resentment and hatred will not make you happier. Even if you believe you are in the right does getting angry or upset to act on an injustice serve your aim to be happier further? In fact getting angry or upset will likely cause more upset in others which could lead to more unhappy feelings for yourself later, for example, guilt, shame, regret, etc. This will push you further away from your aim and desire to be happier.

Pay attention to yourself and your thoughts and take some time to understand what is driving the feelings of anger. They may not be based in truth or what you are actually experiencing now, you may not have all the information and are leaping to judge. No response may be needed at all, instead more observation or information may be required. Alternatively if you feel the feeling of anger is justified wait for the initial emotional reaction to pass or check it as soon as you realise that you are reacting. You can act as if you are angry later once the real anger has subsided, this will be less destructive to your aims of more happiness and being more compassionate to yourself and others.

Example: Stop reading for a couple of minutes. Think about the last time you felt angry and reacted towards somebody else. Do you honestly believe that they set out to make you feel angry and to be on the receiving end of your emotional reactions? Did being angry make you feel any happier in that moment? Did they feel happier at that moment? Did you have to apologise afterwards for your reaction? If you did apologise, did doing that make you feel happier? Did you feel guilt, regret and/or sadness? You can see where this leading with all these unhappy feelings. Be happier... think before you react.

We are often more critical of ourselves than we are of our enemies. A good rule of thumb when it comes to our own internal self critique is to be no more critical of ourselves than we would be of a stranger or a friend.

It is not uncommon for compassion to be viewed as weak, however practising compassion can be a lot tougher than just reacting to a situation. It takes more self control and strength to be patient, listen and respond from a place of self awareness with compassion and understanding.

Enemies and annoying people are a great opportunity to practice and improve your compassionate side. Remember and understand, that they have desires and hopes for being happier just as you but may not be going about finding it in the right way. They may be upsetting many other people while they try to find the right path to happiness. So wish them well on finding their correct path because people can change exactly as you are trying to do now with mindfulness.

Exercising compassion can be one of the most fulfilling parts of being mindful as you are adding to more positivity in the world and making it a happier and more peaceful place for us all to live. Your relationships with others will improve and your relationship with yourself will too. That feels pretty good.

More Kindness

One of the most important attitudes to bring to your mindfulness is kindness. You can be more attentive, present and compassionate but the experience of it can be cold and hard, or you can apply some kindness to it to make it a more warm, caring and gentle experience. By adding kindness to your experiences you can make any moment whether it's positive, negative or neutral just a little bit better.

Example: So you're now wondering what all this actually means and how you can do this. Try looking away from this book for a couple of minutes and keep your focus on just one thing that you can see. Pay attention to it and bring a sense of affection to the way you are looking at it in the same way that you would look into a small child's eyes.

You could try this next time that you eat, in fact try it each time you eat. When the food arrives and before you dive in just take a few moments to notice the smell of the food in the same way you would notice your favourite perfume or aftershave. As you take each bite and chew, notice and savour the different tastes in your mouth and remember how lucky you are to have food that can be enjoyed. Make sure you have chewed and savoured everything in your mouth before have your next helping.

Or as you walk around as part of your day and notice other people, in your head wish them some kindness. Think to yourself "I hope you can be happy" and try to make it come from the heart.

Or try listening to your own negative thoughts with a sense of kindness. Just listen to those thoughts like you would if you were listening to a close friend with some understanding and compassion.

You have unlimited kindness within you, so give it away either to others or to yourself, preferably both. You will notice an effect too, the kinder you are and feel, the more people will be kind to you too. Try it and see for yourself.

More Gratitude

As one of the greatest of all emotions, gratitude can be cultivated easily and studies are starting to show that gratitude improves well-being. Your heart will open when you are aware and grateful for what you do have, instead of what you don't. When you are aware, grateful and open hearted you are more mindful.

Being grateful for what you have involves positive emotions. Unsurprisingly experiencing more positive emotions through showing more gratitude will improve your general well-being and overall positivity.

Recent studies are also showing that you do not need

to express your gratitude to anyone, you just have to feel grateful. Feeling and being grateful for all the things and people that you have in your life and for what they bring to it, will tend to shift your focus away from negative thoughts and feelings, and instead towards more positive thinking.

Once you start being more grateful and start noticing the benefits it becomes like a snowball as you quickly find your are more grateful for anything and everything in your life. Being more grateful and the positive effects it has will also help increase your compassion and kindness.

If you share your gratitude with the person you are grateful to then the benefit is twofold. You feel the positive effects of being grateful and who doesn't like being told that someone else is grateful for what they've done. A great way to do this is using a gratitude letter.

What are you waiting for, show your gratitude to everyone!

2

BENEFITS

NO MATTER HOW MUCH YOU
STRESS OR OBSESS ABOUT
THE PAST OR FUTURE,
YOU CAN'T CHANGE EITHER ONE.
IN THE PRESENT IS WHERE THE
POWER LIES.
BUDDHA

★

To realise the benefits of mindfulness it is important that you turn your mindfulness activities into habits. Habits are easy to do and hard to break because you have created strong neural pathways for them. The more you perform and repeat your mindfulness actions the easier they become, as they become habits.

Repeated studies show that regular practice of mindfulness actually rewires the brain and has been shown to increase levels of serotonin which is vital to happiness. Regular mindfulness practice also reduces levels of the stress related hormone cortisol which contributes to anxiety, depression, memory loss and sleep disorders.

You can also think of each session of mindfulness meditation effectively as a dose, the more you practice, the better the cumulative effects usually are. You can also top up your dosage throughout the day by becoming more aware of the present while you're performing mundane daily acts, like brushing your teeth, doing the dishes, walking the dog, etc.

Calming

Imagine your mind is like an ocean, sometimes it's a rough stormy time and at others the ocean is flat and calm. It doesn't matter what you are doing, thoughts pass through your mind and the weather at the ocean's surface changes reflecting your current thoughts. Practising mindfulness allows you to take a step back and raise yourself out of the water, so you are not affected by whatever the weather conditions are like on the surface of the ocean. From this raised position you can just observe the changes in the ocean surface rather than be controlled by the weather, or actually your own thoughts.

As part of improving your mindfulness skills it is important to remember to focus on being aware of the present using at least one of your senses, sight, hearing, smell, taste and touch. Also make sure you change which sense you use so that you build up the skills and habits with all your senses. Just by maintaining your focus on one of your senses and what they are sensing in the present has a calming effect on your brain.

Also remember that if your mind does wander, it's okay, be kind to yourself, just bring your attention back to your sensing again with the same sense as before. Gradually you'll be able to maintain the focus for longer and receive the calming effect for longer too.

Reduced Stress
As Mindfulness improves emotional regulation the

symptoms of stress can also be alleviated. This in turn leads to a general better mood that also helps combat stressful situations and periods in your life.

Many studies from hundreds of universities are showing that mindfulness not only reduces stress, it also helps prepare you so you cope better during stressful times in your life, helping you to remain happier. As mindfulness makes you more aware of your thoughts you are less likely to take them as literally. Being mindful helps you control your reactions which helps reduce the stress that these can trigger too.

Part of becoming mindful is an increase in emotional intelligence. This will help you better understand other people's emotions and feelings, which in turn should reduce conflicts with others and the negative effects on well-being that this produces. Being mindful also includes showing yourself and others compassion, which will mean you will be less critical and judgemental generally. This will reduce your reactions to situations and the stress that potentially comes with them.

Mindfulness also offers you a way to focus on stressful and depressive thoughts in a different way, enabling you to observe them instead of just feeling them. With a greater understanding of how your own thought patterns are affecting your general state of mind comes an improved well-being, thus improved state of mind.

Reduced Depressive Symptoms

While being mindful and more attentive you are more aware of your body as well as your mind. This helps to detect symptoms that are causes and/or contributing factors of depression a lot sooner so they can be treated or addressed earlier reducing their depressive effects.

Simply being mindful reduces activity in the part of the brain called the amygdala. The amygdala is responsible for producing your stress responses, so being mindful effectively reduces your background stress responses.

Reduced Workplace Stress

Studies are now starting to show that Mindfulness Stress Reduction Training in the workplace is having many positive effects. Participants have reported lower perception of stress, improved emotional and physical health, better sleep and improved self-compassion. Participants are also showing reduced levels of the stress related hormone cortisol in their blood. They have also shown reduced systolic and diastolic blood pressure indicating that they felt less stressed physically and mentally.

This is an area of mindfulness study that is likely to explode over the next few years as businesses start to realise that they can potentially help their employees improve their quality of life overall as well as their productivity at work.

Better Decisions

You are making decisions all day every day whether they are conscious decisions or unconscious decisions. Even deciding to make no decision is a decision. To make a decision, especially a good quality decision you need to be in the right frame of mind. If you are worrying, feeling anxious, stressed or experiencing any other strong emotions or feelings you will not be able to think clearly. This is concerning if you have to make a life changing decision like getting married, whether to buy a new home or change to a new job.

By practising mindfulness you learn to become more aware, attentive and listen to your senses more which will help your decision making. Also apart from providing better clarity to your conscious decision making, you will start to notice that your subconscious contributes to how you make decisions too, through your gut or intuition.

More Attention

Almost everything we do requires a level of of focus and attention of some kind, from reading, writing, driving or even just watching the TV. In an age of the internet, constantly pinging mobile phones and the multi-tasking lives we live now, it seems to be coming at the expense of our attention spans.

One of the main elements of mindfulness meditation is the ability to detect when your mind has wandered off along with the ability to bring it back to the focus of the meditation. As you develop this skill through practising more mindfulness and meditation you will notice improvements in your ability to focus on anything that you are doing, saving you time and improving your sense of achievement when tasks are completed sooner.

Mindfulness intention is to get your mind to focus on only what is happening in the present thus training your brain to focus. As part of mindfulness you accept that your mind will wander off and lose attention from time to time, it also helps train your mind how to quickly refocus too. So by practising mindfulness meditations regularly you will you gain better abilities to maintain focus and be more attentive to the task at hand.

Better General Health

A few minutes of mindful meditation a day can help with your general health and well-being. There is a quickly growing body of evidence that shows several measurable benefits of meditation including, higher brain functioning, increased immune function, lowered blood pressure and lowered heart rate. Regular meditation also demonstrates many psychological changes too, including, increased awareness, increased attention and focus, increased clarity in thoughts and perception, lower anxiety levels, an internal experience of calmness, balance and feeling connected.

Enhanced Ability To Deal With Illness

As with many chronic illnesses, pain management is a big factor that affects the sufferers well-being. Millions of people are living with these types of illnesses all the time along all the associated pain. While traditional pain relief usually involves medication it usually only treats the physical pain and does not try to help with the emotional pain. Suffering with emotional pain will almost definitely have an effect on your well-being.

Most people would rather try to forget about their pain but this creates a state of resistance which itself is stressful. Mindfulness meditation can help create a state of relative calm, balance and a content state even while in physical pain.

Cancer patients and others suffering with other chronic and sometimes terminal conditions are becoming a big focus of studies and in particular, in how mindfulness can help with living with the condition. While mindfulness cannot take away the symptoms of the condition itself, it can help make living with them more manageable. It is starting to show in studies too that caregivers benefit from mindfulness when it comes to the stress and burdens of looking after a loved one.

Better Recovery

Not only can Mindfulness help you deal with and live with the symptoms of a serious illness but it can also help with the recovery too. As mindfulness can improve your general health and reduce stress, it can assist in the recovery of many conditions and illnesses, as you are just generally healthier and less stressed.

Some studies into breast cancer survivors have shown that practising mindfulness, meditation and yoga has enhanced post-traumatic growth (the ability to appreciate life, find meaning and purpose, and see new possibilities from their experience) along with reduced anxiety and stress.

Slower Ageing

Several studies are now showing that practising mindfulness meditations can have an effect of potentially adding years to the life span of the body and improving brain function further into old age. Mindfulness helps with reducing stress and studies are showing that people that suffer with environmental stress and perceived stress may induce premature ageing.

A growing but currently small body of research is showing that the brains degeneration over time may be reduced as meditation helps alter our brain structure and function. The key seems to be continued meditation over time and studies are now trying to work out exactly how much meditation is required. If you consider just a couple of generations ago that the benefits of physical fitness on health, well-being and life span was not generally well known and now many people ensure they play sport and attend gyms on a regular basis for the long term benefits. It seems we are on the edge of realising that mental fitness and regular brain workouts are just as important too.

Reduced Pain

Millions of people live with chronic pain from diseases and injuries. It can not only be a psychical strain but it's an emotional strain too. While traditional medication can alleviate the physical pain it can also increase the emotional pain along with other potential side effects too.

More studies are starting to show that by creating new structures and functional changes in the brain, Mindfulness can help alleviate pain. Many health providers across the world are now seriously considering and already prescribing mindfulness as an alternative or supplement to traditional drug related treatments for chronic pain.

The benefits are most notable in people that have practised mindfulness meditations for over eight weeks generally. Using awareness, kindness, curiosity and acceptance you can bring attention to the pain instead of doing what comes naturally, which is to avoid the pain. Once you are focused on the pain itself you can learn how to differentiate between the physical pain and the psychological pain. Once identified you use mindfulness to let go of the psychological pain leaving only the physical pain.

Better Emotional Understanding

It is impossible to truly be happy, manage or understand happiness without a good foundation of emotional intelligence. Mindfulness requires that you are mindful of your emotions and therefore emotionally aware. With mindfulness you will improve your emotional intelligence which will help you further appreciate your own happiness along with all other emotions you experience.

We are all born with different emotional intelligence levels similar to intellectual intelligence. As with intellectual intelligence, emotional intelligence can be nurtured, cultivated and improved, most notably through practising more mindfulness. A highly emotionally aware individual has learned to accept who they are and that everyone handles emotions differently and are unique.

You physically experience emotions and they partly exist as part of your survival instinct. Anxiety usually manifests itself as a tingling in your stomach while anger will usually manifest as an increase in breathing and heart rate. Your emotions are continuously changing all the time as your experience of the present changes and emotions generally don't last very long.

Emotions happen to you naturally and you can use your mindfulness skills to observe which emotions you are experiencing at any given moment. Generally emotions are perceived as unpleasant, pleasant and neutral and they will likely induce negative or positive feelings in your mind. Mindfulness allows you to observe and accept the emotion you are experiencing without avoiding or reacting to the feelings it induces. Emotional intelligence is a large and interesting subject and certainly worth further investigation once you get deeper into mindfulness.

Better Understanding Of Thoughts

It is important that you do not underestimate the power that your thoughts have. It is now being stated by many that the power of thought is "all powerful". Look around you right now, almost everything you can see started off initially as a thought in somebody's mind. Obviously this does not include nature but even landscapes are modified by man and therefore starts off as a thought in somebody's mind.

These are thoughts that someone or some people persisted with to produce the clothes that you're wearing, the sofa you're sitting on and the building you're sitting in for example. If these people hadn't acted on their initial thoughts that they'd had, that sofa or building may not exist now, or it would, but in a different form because it started from a different thought in maybe a different mind.

Everything you do starts with a thought, from the words you speak, through the actions you perform, and even feelings can be triggered by thoughts. Thoughts are also habit forming, each time you have a new thought, good or bad, a new neural pathway is created in your brain. It is easier for thoughts to take an existing neural pathway than to create a new one, so you are more likely to have the same thought again, which then reinforces the neural pathway and increases the chances of having the thought once more, and so on. Being mindful is key to stopping negative thought patterns becoming habitual in your mind and helps create new neural pathways for hopefully more positive thought patterns.

By being mindful you learn to watch your thoughts, emotions, feelings and actions. This way when you detect negative, untruthful or unhelpful thoughts passing through your mind you can question their validity with kindness and self-compassion. This process alone seems to be enough for your mind to discard them instantly. Just ask yourself, "what of the thoughts I've just been having do I know for sure are actually true?" You won't find many, as most will be assumptions, judgements, imaginary scenarios and more assumptions based upon earlier assumptions.

Good vs Bad Thoughts

As mentioned earlier, it does not matter where you are from in the world, we all have this same drive to be happier in our lives, it is curious though that our mind often seems to try to steer us in the opposite direction. We give more value to negative and bad thoughts than we do to positive and good thoughts and feelings.

Generally a good feeling or thought is a subconscious way of you telling yourself that you like something or it makes you happy. The opposite to this is a bad or negative thought or feeling is your subconscious telling you that you don't like something or it makes you unhappy. If you are going to move in the direction of a happier life then surely you should be listening to these thoughts and feelings as an indicator of direction of travel, which is what most of us do without really realising what's happening.

Here is the problem, when you have a bad or negative thought you often tend to ruminate upon it and as part of that process produce more negative thoughts and consequently more negative feelings. This gives far more value to the original negative thought than it should have had. Whereas when you have a positive, a good thought or feeling you don't tend to spend so much time worrying about it as you would a bad thought, if at all. Someone may pay us several compliments that typically we tend to brush off with a hint of embarrassment without too much thought of again. Yet when the same person makes an observation of us that is negative we don't forget it, we go over it in our minds and may even end up holding it against them for a while.

So now bad thoughts and feelings are given much more weight than good or positive ones. Your instinct is to move further away from whatever is producing the bad or negative feelings and thoughts, and closer towards whatever is producing the good ones. What if a situation, person or decision generates both of these types of thoughts and feelings at times, which is completely normal? Your negative thoughts and feelings tend to be given more weight, so as a result your mind could be tricking you into moving away from something that makes you happier and in turn making you unhappier. We all want to be happier but our mind doesn't always serve as a good judge of whether we are heading in the right direction if left to itself.

As you become more mindful you will be able to better identify these negative thought patterns and the effect they are having on your life judgements and better choose the correct direction of travel for you to be happier. You will also learn to be more grateful for what you do have, reinforce and give more weight to the good thoughts and feelings more. You will also be more compassionate which will help you understand that the negative or bad thought you are having may not be justified or not based on fact before you start giving it so much weight. After all that's what we all want, more of these good and positive feelings and thoughts in our minds to make us feel happier. So always follow the good feelings and give less value to the bad feelings, you will become happier automatically.

3

PREPARATION

TRAIN YOUR MIND TO SEE THE GOOD IN
EVERYTHING. POSITIVITY IS A CHOICE.
THE HAPPINESS OF YOUR LIFE DEPENDS
ON THE QUALITY OF YOUR THOUGHTS.

MARCANDANGEL

Setting Your Intention

Intention

Noun | In - ten – tion

1. What one intends to bring about or do
2. Act in a way with a determination

You will not fully realise the benefits of mindfulness if your intention is not good enough or too vague. It is important not to confuse your intention with a goal or a target. A goal is what you seek to achieve whereas an intention is more the purpose and reason for doing it, along with the attitude that you bring to it.

Your intention should come from the heart and not be goal or target orientated. For example a goal would be something like "I'm being more mindful to lose an amount of weight" whereas an intention could be something like "I'm being more mindful to help myself be more compassionate" or "I'm being more mindful to become stronger emotionally".

Your intention is very important as it is the first step towards becoming and manifesting what it is you want to achieve. Without intention there is no direction or purpose, so setting the correct intention couldn't be more important and will help you focus your mind, heart and soul into bringing it about.

Finding Your Intention

Getting your head around setting your intention isn't always easy when you start thinking about it. There are so many intentions you could choose and probably more than one appeals initially. When choosing what your intention is going to be, make sure it is aligned with your general perspective on life and thoughts about who you are and who you want to be. Be realistic and don't set an intention that is impossible for you to achieve.

How you phrase your intention is almost as important as the actual intention itself. It should always be positive and not include any negative words. It can be a phrase or just a single word. For example it could be "compassion", "love", "peace" or "freedom" and it should not be something like "have less fear" because "less" and "fear" are not positive.

Some common intentions used by others are:

"Health", "Peace", "Love", "Balance", "Courage", "More compassion", "Connect with others", "Feel steady and calm" and "open mind".

Some questions you can ask yourself to help identify what your intention could be:

"What matters most to me right now?"

"What would I like to let go off?"

"What makes me most proud?"

"Who would I like to forgive in my life?"

"What am I grateful for in my life?"

"Which word would I most like to align myself with?"

"Why do I want to be more mindful?"

"What do I want in my life and in the future?"

You should always say to yourself either in your head or out loud what your intention is before you meditate or actively practice mindfulness. The key is to restate your intention whenever you can, especially when you feel you need it, for example, when you are stressed, doubting yourself, etc. It will help you become grounded again and remind you what your focus should be.

Set Your Vision

Your vision is not a goal or an intention, your vision is where you see yourself after a while of being on your mindful journey. You can of course revise your vision after a while of practising mindfulness and you will likely adjust your vision as you realise, understand and experience the benefits of mindfulness yourself. However once you have understood how mindfulness benefits you better you should not change your vision too often as you will lose focus. When you have a consistent vision of where you are going with all your mindfulness efforts, it will be easier to notice what you achieve as you get closer to your vision. Don't change or evolve your vision much once set, otherwise you will never be able to measure how you are doing in getting closer to achieving it.

Obviously as we've seen in previous chapters, mindfulness is primarily about being in the present as much as possible, so giving yourself a vision of the future is a little counter intuitive to what we already know about mindfulness. But by having a vision of where your mindfulness journey will lead you, helps motivate you to keep going and ensure you stay on the correct path and direction towards your vision.

You may find it easier to set a vision after you have

been doing mindfulness for a while and better understand what it has to offer. A good trick once you know what your vision is, is to write it out on a piece of paper and pin it somewhere where you will see it often and be reminded of what it is. Your vision could be of a period a long way in the future or it could be something closer. Who do you see yourself as in ten years time for example?

Who Are You Doing This For?

Ultimately you should be practising mindfulness for yourself, however as you start to notice the differences that mindfulness brings in yourself, so will the others around you. So it's not a bad idea to consider who in your life will see the benefits that mindfulness will bring for you. It might help setting your intention and vision too. Consider who is in your life and how they would also benefit when you start to realise the benefits of mindfulness.

The more mindfulness you practice the more likely you will be more kind, compassionate and attentive to others. You will likely be less irritable and more approachable. Just some people who will likely benefit from you being more mindful are:

- Family

- Partner / spouse
- Friends
- People you work with
- Neighbours

As mentioned earlier though, you must be setting off on your mindfulness journey purely for yourself and for the benefits it will bring for you alone. The benefits and the better relationships you will likely have with others as a result should be considered a very welcome bonus. It's time to put yourself first but being aware that others will likely receive some benefit will help you feel less selfish.

Be Committed

When you start off on this new journey into practising mindfulness one of your biggest questions is probably going to be about how committed you will need to be and how much time you will need to put aside for it. In short, the more you put in, the more you will get out.

Becoming more mindful and realising all the benefits that it can bring to your life will ultimately require you to change the way that you think and see the world you live in. This cannot be achieved overnight and will take as long as it takes. The more you do, the quicker it will happen, but you need to remember that your mind has had all these years to build up it's current habits and ways of thinking that will be changing to a more mindful attitude and outlook.

It takes time to undo and replace your current way of thinking but the biggest key to becoming more mindful is regular and consistent commitment to mindfulness. So you should be ready to put aside some time each day for mindfulness. How much time that is and when it is, is entirely up to you and can range from a couple of minutes to half an hour a day or maybe even more. As mentioned earlier, the more you do the bigger and quicker the benefits.

Each day you will gradually start to change and notice that the way you think and experience your world is changing slightly. With each day there is more change as your new habits start to form. You should be prepared to commit eight weeks to fully notice the change but you'll likely notice changes in yourself and how other people interact with you very quickly.

Spread The Word

When you start on your new mindfulness journey it may help to keep you motivated by telling those who are close to you, like family and loved ones what you are doing. However it is probably better that you do not tell them of the changes they are likely to see in you so you do not build up expectations and so they and you are pleasantly surprised.

Once you start noticing the differences in yourself and your well-being, you may also feel compelled to share this new found wisdom you have with your friends, family and colleagues and wax on about how it could improve their lives as much it has yours. This is not uncommon and many of us have these urges to spread the word of mindfulness and the benefits it could bring to the many of the people we care about.

However, we've all been on the receiving end of a friends lecture about how wonderful their latest fad is and how much better we would be too if we got involved as well. Although it comes from a caring place, it's often done in a way that's overzealous and in a pushy manner, and often feels more like a criticism of how we are living our lives already.

So here is another opportunity to be more mindful and show some kindness, compassion and less judgment. Probably the best way to handle these situations is to wait until someone else asks what has prompted the difference they've noticed in you. Close friends, family and work colleagues are all likely to pick up your new outlook and demeanour and question you about how it's come about.

Remember to be kind and be grateful for their interest, making sure that before you launch into how they should get into practising mindfulness too, that they are actually wanting to know more. Be attentive to how they are reacting to what you are telling them, they could be just pleased that you've made some improvements and may not necessarily be that interested how you've done it.

It is important to also remember that mindfulness is not a "cure all" and people's issues and problems are often a lot more complicated than they seem on the surface. Sometimes people will not be interested in what mindfulness has to offer or may not always see the benefits to their own situation by practising it.

Also remember not to judge them and assume you know how being more mindful could help them. Once they've noticed the difference in you and you've explained how it's not that difficult to achieve, you can point them to the right resources, like this book, to help them find out for themselves whether it will be suitable for them after their own research.

Psychical Exercise

By being more mindful while performing physical exercise you are more likely to feel the benefit of the exercise and gain far more enjoyment while doing it. You will also likely feel the benefits of the enjoyment afterwards too. Being mindful of the physical activity that you are doing while you are doing it will help your attention stay focused on improving your skill level and ability instead of worrying about something else, like the report that has to be finished at work or what you are doing after.

Mindfulness will likely positively affect you psychologically and physically too. It will help to improve your breathing rate and depth along with improving heart rate and muscular activity as well. Research is starting to show that those who practice mindfulness tend to suffer with less effects of stress and in turn have a more positive attitude towards the health benefits of physical activities. Those practising mindfulness are shown to also be better at setting intentions for physical activity including being better at planning and preparing for it.

Mindfulness can also help with performance too as not only will you likely be attending more sessions due to being less tired and fatigued through stress, but as you are more attentive you will more likely understand your body's sensations better. This should help achieve maximum levels of performance and help you enjoy your chosen activity more.

You can informally include mindfulness into your psychical activity by just being in the present moment. Making sure that you are fully focused on the current point, current play or simply watching your breathing and how it changes when your level of activity changes. There are lots of ways you can integrate mindfulness into just about all physical activities and not just sport. It could also be your intention for starting your mindfulness practice too.

Having The Right Attitude

One of the most important factors that will influence whether mindfulness will work for you is your attitude. If you believe mindfulness is hard work and takes too much effort then you will not see the real benefits it has to offer you. Once you understand how easy mindfulness actually is and realise that even when you do make mistakes, being mindful allows you to let the mistakes go. By doing this, your attitude will likely change and improve.

When it comes to your attitude towards your

mindfulness practice, the easiest attitude to probably aim for is a neutral attitude of neither good or bad. Instead an attitude of acceptance and acknowledgement is preferred, you will be as good as you can be at practising your mindfulness and understanding that you are doing your best and this is acceptable. Getting frustrated and annoyed when your mind wanders will cause you to focus less on your mindfulness and just make it harder for yourself. Instead, accept that this happens to everyone and is just part of the process. Remember, any amount of mindful thought is more than you were doing before and is having a positive effect and benefit.

Mindfulness is about experiencing the present moment as much as possible and even if you feel that you are becoming annoyed because of a wandering mind, or an outside source is interfering with your focus, you are being mindful as you are noticing how you feel right now.

If you can't focus and your mind keeps returning to the same thoughts then you have an opportunity to use mindfulness to investigate these thoughts further and why you are thinking them right now. Are they based on something you know to be true or is your mind telling you stories? Are these thoughts making you feel something right now? What is that feeling? Are you experiencing emotions in your body at the moment? In your mind ask yourself similar mindful questions which will help bring you into a more mindful frame of mind and will probably help stop the thought cycle you were previously having, allowing you to focus better on your mindful practice.

As with asking the questions of yourself above, curiosity is the easiest way to become more mindful. The act of being curious causes you to use your senses and mind to understand something and that is in itself being mindful. Whether you are just looking closer at something, listening more intently or thinking about something to understand it better. If you investigate more you will automatically become more mindful, realising this alone will help your attitude. You can use curiosity to be more mindful while performing daily tasks like brushing your teeth or having a shower. Can you really the taste minty flavour and the texture of your toothpaste. While showering, feel the temperature of the water on different parts of your body, try to smell the scents and aromas of your shower gel and shampoo.

Another way to help with your attitude is to practice letting go of any negative emotions, feelings or thoughts about your mindfulness practice. Use your curiosity to investigate what negative emotions you experience when you practice mindfulness, observe them as they play out and try to understand why you are experiencing them right now. Once you've done this, allow yourself to let those emotions run their course and start using the same technique to analyse related feelings and thoughts. Keep working through these and keep letting go until you get to the source of what you are experiencing, you will almost definitely find its not related to your actual mindfulness practice and this whole process was mindful itself.

Forgive And Let Go

It is pretty much impossible to live life without getting hurt at some point, often through no fault of our own. Yet even though it may not be our fault we often carry around resentment and hate from that hurt for months, years and sometimes a lifetime. While we carry this around it affects our decisions, attitudes, confidence, self esteem and weighs us down, stopping us enjoying life to the full. Having unresolved emotional pain affects us when we experience something similar again too, as repressed emotional pain keeps accumulating which is certainly not mindful.

A couple of key things to remember are, it doesn't matter how much resentment or hate you hold inside for another person or situation you are the only person feeling that resentment and hate. In fact, it is probably likely the other person gives it no thought at all any more, so it's only yourself you hurt with the hate and resentment. You may be in the right now and maybe you were in the right at the time but the only person feeling this resentment and anger is you and holding onto it for longer just prolongs your own pain.

Also by allowing yourself to forgive someone or a situation for which you are still carrying this resentment and hate does not mean you need to forget how it made you feel at the time, and they certainly don't need to know that they've been forgiven. All you are doing is giving yourself the gift of forgiveness which allows you to let go of the resentment, anger and pain you've been carrying around all this time. You are doing this purely for you. This will allow you to be happier, have better well-being and allow you to be more mindful in similar situations, judging them purely and fairly on what you are experiencing in the present moment, instead of bringing previous unresolved emotional pain to an unrelated moment.

By doing this you are being kind and compassionate to

yourself which is important for mindfulness. You will also enable yourself to feel happier as you will not be ruminating any more and causing yourself more pain and anguish with thoughts about the past. Take back control of your own feelings, thoughts and emotions and give yourself the power to control how you feel about this. It doesn't matter how badly you've been hurt, stopping the other person or situation making you feel this way over and over again is the best form of retribution.

It does take practice and time to be able to forgive and shift your attitude but the more mindfulness you practice the easier it becomes. You could initially start on something smaller that affects you and build up to the bigger causes of pain as you become more proficient at it. You must forgive with kindness, compassion and genuinely mean it and remember the only person you are doing this for, is you, nobody else.

4

CONTROL

IT ALL BEGINS AND
ENDS IN YOUR MIND.
WHAT YOU GIVE POWER TO,
HAS POWER OVER YOU
LEON BROWN

For some people, life is a wonderful joyous adventure, while for many others it's a life of stress, anxiety, resentment and disappointment. In many cases the only difference between these people is how they deal with their challenges, face their fears and how they cope with stress of stressful situations we all encounter from time to time. Basically the difference is just how they think and how they manage their own emotions and feelings.

Some people take adversity and problems as a chance to learn and grow while for others it can be the end of their world. Those who seem to enjoy a good quality of life regardless of whatever the world throws at them tend to be more in control of their emotions and do not let emotions and feelings control them.

It's a common misconception that mindfulness is about letting go of control. It's easy to see why when so many mindfulness books and guides actually say that less control is part of being mindful. Too much emphasis is often placed on this as it's both true, but more false as many parts of mindfulness require lots of control, especially in the early stages of learning mindfulness. Those who are in control of their thoughts and focus are usually dwelling less in the past and fretting less about the future too, they are more in the present and mindful.

Some of us are able to think in this more positive manner usually due to our upbringings, however everyone is capable of having these positive thought patterns and mindfulness is a very big step in the right direction. When you start trying to be more mindful it seems that it requires lots of control of your thoughts to start with, but very quickly it becomes second nature and you don't realise that you are doing it a lot of the time. As you start taking control of those negative thoughts you will notice the benefits to your general well-being and outlook very quickly.

The paradox missed by a lot mindfulness books is that the very act of letting go of some control itself requires control over your mind to make this happen. So if you can't let go of your inner control freak, don't panic, there is plenty to control when being mindful.

What Is Control

Control is to exercise or influence change on something to make it what you want it to be. If you want to give up control of something you need to:

- Understand what state of mind you are in now
- Know or recognise what the state of "no

control" is
- You must be able to change (control) your state of mind.

Without any of these elements you can't give up control.

Mindfulness requires that we direct our attention and focus to the present moment. This requires that you control your attention. First you need to understand where your attention is currently, either in the past, present or future. Once you have recognised your attention is in the past or future you need to consciously change it (control it) to the present.

By taking control of your mind a bit more than you currently do, you will start to realise that thoughts are events that only occur in your head and not in real life. We all have thoughts that conjure up emotions and feelings that are sometimes good or sometimes bad but by realising that these are feelings and emotions triggered by our own mind's thoughts and not external events or experiences in the present you are taking control.

You can exercise control by mentally choosing whether to let these thoughts affect you emotionally too.

Imagine sitting at a bus stop, as you sit there lots of "thought" buses are passing you by. When you are in control you can choose which bus to board and which buses to just let pass.

Loss Of Control Common Symptoms

- **Poor emotional awareness** If you cannot identify which emotions are triggering specific feelings within your mind you are unlikely to be able to control and inhibit a resulting reaction.

- **Poor emotional clarity** Emotions can often be combined with others to create an "emotional cocktail". If you cannot identify and differentiate between emotions that are being experienced together you will likely lack the control to inhibit the reactions of one or more of these emotions.

- **Non acceptance of reaction to emotions** If you cannot accept how a reaction is related to a specific emotion or feeling then it is impossible to control and inhibit the reaction.

- **Disrupted goals or plans** The lack of ability

to control and inhibit reactions can lead to disruption of your life goals and plans likely causing more negative emotions.

- **No control strategies** Often many of us lack control strategies that can help identify likely upcoming reactions. With awareness of some simple strategies control of reactions can be easily achieved.

Reacting vs Responding

We spend much of our time just reacting to events and others in our lives. As a reaction tends to be an instinctive action or a gut reaction often based upon fears, insecurities and vulnerabilities, they tend to feature little or no thought. As this is not usually the most appropriate, rational or logical way to act it often leads to unhappy results that make the current situation worse. You will never be able to remove people and events from your life so there will always be times when something or someone will bother you enough to cause a reaction, but what you should be striving to achieve now, is how to respond in a thoughtful, calm, compassionate and cooperative manner instead of just thoughtlessly reacting.

By being mindful more often you are more likely to

earlier identify emotions as they start to build and be prepared to control a resulting reaction more effectively. In an ideal world you can totally inhibit any negative reactions, but even just being mindful enough to identify that you are reacting will often be enough for you to be able stop the reaction continuing and limit any potential damage.

A level of emotional intelligence is required to be able to identify and distinguish between emotions. However most of us have enough emotional intelligence to know whether the emotions being experienced at any given time feel good or bad. Knowing that you're feeling a bad emotion is a sign that you should be preparing to control a bad reaction that may follow.

Controlling emotional reactions requires an intention to do so. If you have no intention to control your reactions you effectively hand control of those reactions to other people or outside events. You are effectively walking around the world we all live in out of control! You may believe that you are in control when you react, if this is the case, you can easily prove this to yourself by choosing not to react next time. If you cannot inhibit the reaction, you are not in control.

You may not believe that reacting is a bad thing. It's true, sometimes a reaction does not have any negative effects and may even result in a positive outcome. However if you are not inhibiting your reactions you are removing any control over the outcomes to your reactions altogether.

While you are reacting, you often become irrational and you cannot think with enough clarity to assess whether the reaction is proportional and warranted. By exercising control to inhibit the reaction you are not surrendering your option to respond in the same way as you would have reacted, you are just ensuring you are considering how to respond to achieve the outcome you ultimately want.

By being more mindful and being present more often you are more likely to identify situations that will lead to emotions that have reactions that need controlling. As you are paying more attention to the current moments you are less likely to be caught out or surprised by situations that will trigger these kind of emotions and consequently their reactions. Being mindful will more likely lead to you changing the course of conversations and actions through being kinder, less judgmental and more compassionate.

Mindfulness offers several ways you can better control the reactions to your emotions.

Meditation

Meditation while easy is possibly the most difficult element of mindfulness to get your head around for most of us. I'm sure you have lots thoughts about how you don't have enough time to do it and how it's a bit too hippy and possibly just not for you. It doesn't need to take long and the benefits you gain far out way any time spent meditating.

A common misconception is that meditating is the same as relaxing. It is not, meditating is relaxing but just relaxing does not have the same benefits as meditating. Unlike meditation, relaxing does not control your mind from having the thoughts it wants to have. Often when you are just relaxing because your mind is not consumed with an activity that keeps it mindful, relaxing can be a time when you are less in control of your mind because control is relaxed too. Of course we all need to relax but do not believe relaxing is the same as mediation, in fact, relaxing is closer to being the opposite to meditating in terms of helping control your thoughts.

Meditating will help you reach an improved state of

self awareness and when practised regularly also has many other proven benefits too, like improving memory and relief of the some less severe symptoms of anxiety and depression.

Meditation is discussed later in the book in more detail but by improving your self awareness generally through regular meditation it will become a lot easier to control your reactions and feelings.

Letting Go

We all experience positive and negative emotions from time to time like anger, sadness, happiness, excitement to name just a few. The key is to observe them and not judge yourself for having such emotions and feelings. By being more self aware and observing your emotions more, you will learn what each emotion feels like for you and be able to categorise them appropriately.

By understanding which emotions you are experiencing you will be able to realise that emotions pass relatively quickly if they are just observed, acknowledged and then accepted. Once you've accepted that the emotion you are feeling is perfectly reasonable for the circumstances you find yourself in the present moment, you can just let it go instead of reacting. Once that emotion has passed you can choose an appropriate response if one is warranted.

Self Awareness

As you are probably starting to see now, mindfulness is really about being as aware of the present moment as you can be, whether that's internal or external to you. It's not always easy to start with, but the more you practice the easier it becomes and consequently the easier you'll find life becomes.

Another thing you should be aware of is that practising mindfulness is an ongoing journey. It is not something you practice until you believe you've overcome a particular issue, as you'll gradually revert back to old habits if you stop. Consider, we are all born as mindful newborn babies that experience the world for the very first time. They have no choice other than to be focused on the present, yet here you are now trying to learn something you found easy when you were born.

Something to be aware of, it doesn't matter how much mindfulness you practice, you will still feel emotions like anger, sadness, unhappiness. However, you will be able to recognise them without reacting and be able to let them go. This will help stop you from hanging onto the emotional feelings and whatever triggered them for any longer than you need to, so they don't continue to bring you down. Soon with practice you will be judging yourself and others less, along with more kindness which will improve your quality of life, provide you with more control over your thoughts without becoming overwhelmed with emotions.

Learning To Respond

Pause. The most important thing to remember that by being mindful whenever you detect that you are going to react, pause. The old saying of "counting to ten" is true because it gives you some thinking and mindful time. This thinking time should be used to further use your mindfulness skills to become fully aware of exactly what is going on in the present moment, think and assess what your next move (response) should be.

The pause should last for as long as you feel the need to react. Usually this is only for a few seconds but if it takes a bit longer then just wait. Remember even though you may believe you are completely in the right, your reaction could give away any advantage or high ground you currently have. Pausing and then responding with intelligence, compassion and a calmness will better serve the outcome that you desire.

As your mindfulness skills improve you will find it easier to pause in these situations. If you do not get it right don't worry. If you are still reacting and you realise that you forgot to pause, pause at this point, this will at least stop any further reaction and any more damage being done. If you forgot to pause and the reaction has passed, again don't worry, just resolve yourself to learn from this situation. Understand what happened to trigger the reaction and ensure you are paying attention when similar circumstances arise in the future, so you can pause next time.

5

BEING HAPPIER YOU

YOU CAN'T CONTROL
THE WAVES,
BUT YOU CAN
LEARN TO SURF.
JON KABAT-ZINN

Many of us are brought up to believe that our happiness is related and linked to possessions, relationships and events, however these are all external to us. True happiness comes from within ourselves and is a result of being loving and compassionate to ourselves. Happiness comes from the love you share with others and the gratitude for what you have and not what you don't have.

A mentality of not being happy until you get what you want will mean you are unlikely to be truly happy as we always want more than we have - it's human nature. There is nothing wrong with wanting and aspiring for more but what you want in the future should not determine whether you are happy now. You can be happy now and still want and desire more things, relationships and experiences.

Most of us don't realise that happiness is a choice and is entirely down to us. We choose whether we are happy or unhappy in any given moment. Mindfulness will help you realise that by showing yourself love, compassion and gratitude and the same to others, brings happiness to the present moment. Happiness really is an inside job, make yourself happier right now by showing some love, kindness or gratitude - give it away, it's all free!

Feel Less Anxious

Almost all of us suffer with anxiety at sometime or another, yet for some it is a constant problem that never seems to go away. When one issue to feel anxious about has passed, there is another one waiting in the queue, or there are multiple issues that cause anxiety at the same time. Feeling anxiety about feeling anxious can also be a problem too.

Having a problem with anxiety can come from seemingly nowhere, can be very debilitating, last for many years and for many suffering with repeated bouts of anxiety it can feel like it will always be in their life. Mindfulness combined with self compassion can offer some well needed relief from anxiety and for some it can really be a complete life changer.

There are many factors or combination of factors that can influence whether you will feel anxious in a given moment, including, the current situation you are experiencing, previous life experiences, your genes, caffeine, alcohol and drugs to name a few. Anxiety is an emotion that triggers feelings of worry and tension, along with increasing your blood pressure. As with fear it is intended to help protect us from harm but often in the lives we live nowadays it is often a misplaced emotion, however real it feels at the time.

Worrying thoughts that tend to fuel themselves with more worrying thoughts create a negative thought pattern that finally results in feeling anxious. The more you worry the worse the worrying becomes. The main way that mindfulness helps with anxiety is to allow you to first identify that you are having these worrying thoughts in the present moment and then to befriend them. You will learn through being more mindfully present that these thoughts and worries will pass on their own if left alone. You will understand that they are just thoughts and are usually not based in reality or based upon fact.

What mindfulness teaches us is to understand what we are feeling and experiencing in the present moment whether it is good or bad. Instead of avoiding or trying to push worrying and anxious thoughts to the back of your mind, mindfulness encourages us to take some curiosity and apply some self compassion to these thoughts and feelings. If you try avoiding or push away worrying or anxious thoughts they tend to come back stronger, giving them more control over your life. Mindfulness helps you look at them with kindness and understanding of what they are, helping you to stop them getting out of control.

Worrying a lot is usually a way of avoiding emotions of

fear. Worrying and anxiety could be your way of not dealing with the underlying deeper emotions of fear, hence why the worrying continues. Mindfulness will help look closer at what you are actually feeling and experiencing in the moment, which will help you identify and understand that feelings and emotions pass. You will learn that by letting them go they will subside and change to another feeling or emotion if not focused upon.

By using your Mindfulness skills you can develop a healthier understanding of your emotions and feelings. By looking closer and trying to understand exactly what you are experiencing in the moment instead of trying to avoid them, you can challenge your thoughts and worries and allow the emotions and feelings to pass without causing more anxiety and with less struggle.

Enjoy More Laughter

As a result of being more mindful and less caught up in your thoughts you'll be more in the present, which means that you get to enjoy the present a lot more when it's good. Mindfulness helps improve your general well-being too and makes you more likely to be happier with whatever life throws at you, along with being able fully appreciate all the good feelings when they come.

To be able to laugh at something you need to be present in the current moment to appreciate how funny it is, this is where being mindful comes in. If you are away in your mind or start analysing whatever it is that's makes you laugh, it is not funny any more.

Studies have shown that laughing increases endorphins in the brain and they can help reduce physical pain too. After all, they do say "laughter is the best medicine." So prescribe yourself a laughter break when you are starting to notice some negative thoughts or feelings if you can, it will help. You can also try holding a smile for up to two minutes. This has also been shown to improve how you feel and most people will feel the benefit in less than two minutes.

Enjoy More Tears

It might sound a bit odd to say that you will enjoy more tears but having more tears will bring you more enjoyment overall. Many of us have problems when it comes to letting ourselves have a good cry, mainly due to the way we are brought up and made to feel that crying is a sign of weakness. Obviously tears are usually brought on by feeling sadness and for many of us, feeling sadness is also linked to feeling like a failure in some way. Many of us don't cry enough, repressing sad feelings and ending up carrying them around with us and allowing them to affect our daily lives and experiences in ways they really shouldn't.

In many cases we may cry a little and stop ourselves due to embarrassment and fears of being perceived as weak, a failure or just over emotional. This stops us fully experiencing the feeling in full and completely. By being mindful of your emotions and feelings you will learn that to cry is one of the best ways to release the feelings of sadness from within you.

You will also be able to understand that when you do have a good cry, you'll know that you've helped to completely experience the sadness in full without any remaining after effects. Once the sadness has fully passed you can use you mindfulness to experience emotions and feelings that are happier instead of always carrying around deeper feelings of sadness. Effectively, more tears now equates to more time for joy later.

Experience Greater Confidence

Practising mindfulness enables you to experience more of the present moment along with the feelings and thoughts that you are having at that time. This enables you to notice negative thoughts and negative thought patterns that don't serve your self-esteem and confidence well. You will also understand what you need in this moment enabling you to make better choices which will reinforce your confidence and improve your self-esteem.

Even by just adding small doses of mindfulness into your life can help calm your mind, so you can be more aware of the confidence busting thought patterns and break free of them. Obviously practising mindfulness will not stop whatever events life has to throw at you but it will help you better respond to those events and that will help build your confidence and self-esteem.

When you have low self-esteem and confidence you will likely find yourself apologising to others for things that are not actually your fault or just to make them feel better. Often this can make you look and feel weaker along with damaging your self-esteem and confidence. Using your mindfulness skills to help notice when you are about to apologise, so you can pause while you determine whether you have anything to apologise for. Unless you actually inconvenienced someone or did something wrong, just acknowledge that something uncomfortable has occurred and remind yourself you didn't do anything that required an apology. Obviously if an apology is required then make sure you take responsibility and apologise with empathy, compassion and honesty.

Do you notice that sometimes you gossip about and judge others in a negative way? Talking about other people in this way will make you look and feel insecure. Confident people do not do this as they are secure enough to know that it makes them feel bad and look bad. Use your mindfulness skills to identify when you are about to start talking about someone else in this way, ask yourself, "what does this achieve for me and how I will feel?".

Another confidence zapping trait is not being able to accept a compliment. Some of us shut down and feel uncomfortable when someone pays us a compliment which is another indication of low self-esteem. Being more mindful will help you identify these feelings in the moment that you receive the compliment so you can simply realise that all that is required is a pleasant "thank you" which will make the other person know you appreciate the compliment and assist in raising your self-esteem.

Another common indicator of a lack of confidence in social situations is using your mobile telephone as a distraction tool. Obviously we all receive messages and emails that need to be attended to at some point and some do require immediate action, but if you find yourself continually checking for new messages or emails, it may be a sign of feeling uncomfortable. Looking like you are busy attending to emails or messages also makes you harder to approach and if people don't engage with you because you look too busy, this will also have an effect on your confidence. Simply put your phone away and allow yourself to check it periodically but not continually. Use your mindfulness skills to assess the people around you and work out who seems friendly and approachable. Being more mindful will be helping your general well-being anyway and making you more approachable too.

People that have low self-esteem don't realise that they look insecure to other people. By simply trying to be more mindful and address some of these confidence damaging traits like those described above will actually help boost your confidence on its own. The more you appear confident, the more you will feel confident as other people react to your confident behaviour and words. This is one area where "faking it until you make it" in a mindful way can really help.

Enjoy Better Sleep

There are many factors that affect the quality of your night time sleep and we've all experienced sleepless nights, with the debilitating effects the next day and for many this is a recurring problem. It is claimed that prolonged poor sleep quality can lead to issues with mental health and can also manifest itself in your physical health too. Anxiety, stress and worry are often major causes of not getting a good night's sleep or waking up earlier than you need.

Several studies have shown that people practising mindfulness suffer less with insomnia, have improved sleep quality and suffer less with impairment during the day. By being mindful even while you are trying to sleep you will be able to identify the negative thought patterns, worries and anxious feelings. Observe them with a kindness and self-compassion that allows you to relax and sleep.

You can also easily practice your mindfulness before bed ensuring you are thinking about the present moment instead of worrying about the days events or what is going to happen tomorrow before you get into bed. For example mindfully brush your teeth or mindfully take a bath or a shower. Obviously make sure you do not use your phone before bed too.

A good night's sleep will also help your mindfulness practice too, as sleep deprivation reduces your emotional regulation. Whereas being more mindful will increase your emotional regulation. Reduced emotional regulation will lead to poorer choices and decisions and will likely make you more reactive, making practising your mindfulness more challenging.

Gain Improved Resilience

Life throws many things at us to make it more challenging but by just being more mindful you can cope and bounce back quicker and with less effort, allowing you more time to enjoy life. As you become aware that you can cope and bounce back from things that go wrong quicker, you will also become less anxious about upcoming issues as result.

When something goes wrong in life you can often end up experiencing a barrage of emotions and feelings, some that you may not experience often, if ever before. Mindfulness helps you observe these feelings and emotions to better understand them, experience them and then let them go.

There are several ways you can help yourself become more resilient for when things go wrong in life, many of which regular mindfulness practice will help with. A mindful person tends to cultivate close, supportive and positive relationships with others that help when challenging times arise. They also tend to try to find a positive to take from the situation when something goes wrong or against the plan. Mindful people tend to better understand themselves and their needs, resulting in a more positive approach to issues.

Use your mindfulness skills to focus on positive and optimistic thoughts and feelings, remember being positive is a choice. Learn to be more decisive and take action, this will save you from ruminating on which is the best decision to take. Finally, just accept that bad things happen to all of us and it is just part of life. You will cope if you use your mindfulness skills to best understand what you are experiencing in the present and you will likely learn a lot more about yourself as part of the process.

Eat Better

Bringing mindfulness and a better awareness of taste, smell, texture and the look of your food that you are putting into your body, should help you notice that the way you experience meal times changes for the better in many ways, without you having to put in any real effort. Mindfulness brings an attention, intention and awareness to what you are eating at meal times and the experiences that different foods can give you.

As you are mindful about everything, including what you eat, you'll probably start to notice that you become gradually more adventurous when it comes to what you choose from the menu or cook at home. You'll probably start to realise that always eating the same foods is quite boring and that there are so many wonderful tastes and experiences out there for you to try.

You might also start to wonder about the journey the food you are putting into your body has taken to get to your plate. You may also wonder about how processed the food is and whether it is healthy for you. Using mindfulness after a meal will tell you more about how eating the food has made you feel and it could be that you start to make changes to your diet overall.

Typically in the lives we lead nowadays it is all too easy to gulp down a plate of food in front of the TV without even noticing half of it and whether you actually needed to eat it all. If you are mindful when you eat you will take longer to enjoy your plate of food and savour every mouthful. You will be better at detecting when you are full and less likely to overeat. Overeating when done on a regular basis will lead to issues with your weight and health.

Reduce Ego

We all have one and simply the ego is our own sense of identity, self esteem and self importance. It exists purely in our own minds and is generally false. It's based upon our self beliefs of who we are, our personality, our traits and our perceived abilities. It is a mental construction of ourselves and our own self image. When your thoughts start with "I" or "me" it is your ego talking to you. Your ego can make you feel positive or negative about anything but an overly positive or a negative ego will not help you be or remain happy.

Mindfulness allows you to observe your thoughts and feelings without judgements and reactions and know that many of these are just products of your own mind or ego. Being mindful allows you to witness your ego without being controlled by it. Once you can see the show that your ego produces in your mind you can start to influence and now direct the performances instead of being controlled by them.

Become Kinder

Most of us care and are kind to those we know and are close to, however many of us don't give ourselves the same kindness and care. Often we are more critical of ourselves than we would be of those we care about if they were faced with the same circumstances or situation. It's all too easy to brood over something that has happened in the past, what could happen in the future, judging ourselves, worrying or comparing ourselves to others when we could be spending that time caring and being kind to ourselves instead.

Most of us know how to be kind when needed yet we need to learn that we can do this for ourselves too. Fortunately kindness to oneself can be learned. Using mindfulness you can identify negative thoughts and feelings as they arise, learn and experience the act of sending kindness and compassion to those thoughts and feelings. The better that you become at giving yourself kindness you will notice that you start to feel warm, relaxed, calmer and ultimately happier.

As you are being mindful you will also better understand how your kindness affects you and your feelings in these moments and it will help you better understand how it affects others too. Some simple ways to offer yourself some kindness are to soften your self talk, place a hand over your heart, cuddle something or yourself and make sure you smile (even if forced). All of these simple but effective actions will help you feel a bit kinder to yourself.

Have More Gratitude

By being more grateful for what you have now will automatically push your mind in a positive direction. When you really appreciate what you have in your life now, you will start to feel happier. Of course we all want more in our lives but how often do you really take stock and feel the gratitude for what you have already. Our brains have a tendency to focus on the negative aspects of life, yet by just being more grateful for what you have you can change this to thoughts of joy, love and contentment very quickly.

Research is starting to show that by being generally more grateful that not only is mental health improved but also improves your sleep quality and the amount of sleep you experience. Key to using gratitude to improve your well-being and making yourself feel happier is to be grateful each day. Spend a few minutes each day being thankful and grateful for what you have in your life and for what life has given you. Ideally do this in the morning so you start the day in a positive frame of mind. You should start to notice increased feelings of optimism and satisfaction with life.

You will probably find when you really start to think about all the things in your life that there is to be grateful for that the list can be very long, which is an encouraging start. Try focusing on one thing, person, situation or area of your life and start thinking about how grateful you are for all the different elements. Try to pick a different subject each time and before you know it you will be grateful for hundreds of things in your life.

Some good places to start are, think of someone that has helped you in your life, all that they have done for you and all the positive results that have come about because of this. Think about all the people that have helped your dinner get to your plate and be grateful for all that they all have done along each step of it's journey to your stomach. The list of things to be grateful will be endless as with each moment that passes there is something else to be grateful for. This is one of the quickest ways you can improve your mood, so what are you waiting for, feel some gratitude now.

6

BEING HAPPIER IN RELATIONSHIPS

AWARENESS IS LIKE THE SUN.
WHEN IT SHINES ON THINGS,
THEY ARE TRANSFORMED.
THICH NHAT HANH

It's not difficult to see that having the qualities that mindfulness encourages within a relationship of any kind can only enhance it. Mindfulness encourages less judging, more attentiveness, more compassion and more empathy to name but a few. When it comes to romantic relationships new research is starting to show that higher levels of mindfulness can lead to more satisfying and happier relationships. Practising Mindfulness over a period of time creates changes within the brain that makes us better relationship partners.

Inside the brain, the amygdala is the brains threat detection centre and is responsible for the flight or fight response. Also inside the brain is the prefrontal-cortex which is responsible for calming us down from anger or fear and stopping us from getting into negative thought patterns that spiral out of control. Mindfulness practice is shown to reduce the size of the amygdala, thus reducing the sensitivity of the fight or flight response. It is also shown that mindfulness practice strengthens the prefrontal-cortex keeping us more in control. These two factors help us to be more aware in a disagreement or an argument of what is helpful and not helpful at that point.

Furthermore, mindfulness practice is also shown to

strengthen the anterior cingulate cortex inside the brain which is associated with self-perception, regulation of emotions, attention and impulses. This part of the brain is also related to how well you can see problems from another perspective and helps you adapt to more flexible views of you and your partner.

Many of us bring emotional traumas from our pasts and vulnerabilities to relationships which can cause us to get stuck into negative patterns and repeat behaviours relationship after relationship. Romantic relationships are especially good at exposing vulnerabilities and distrust. Mindfulness practice helps us to be calmer, be more adaptable and view the moments in the relationship for what they actually are. Mindfulness allows us to better understand what feelings and issues are related to the actual relationship and which are caused by outside influences, such as work related stress, family issues, etc.

Staying with the science for a bit longer. Mindfulness practice helps create positive changes in the insula area of the brain which is responsible for emotional awareness and empathy. The better your insula functions the better you will be at understanding your own feelings and relating to your partner's feelings.

Mindfulness helps us focus on being more open and accepting of our partner and their flaws. If we find ourselves focusing too much on their flaws we can choose to focus on their more positive attributes instead. We better understand that our partners behaviour may be less based upon us and more based upon the previous life experiences and traumas making us more forgiving and helping improve emotional intimacy and a stronger connection between both.

So one of the main benefits of your mindfulness practice could be that it just improves and makes you happier in your romantic relationship. If you both start practising mindfulness regularly then things can only improve from where you are now for both of you.

Listen With More Attentiveness

One of the skills that can be developed with regular mindfulness practice is more active listening and a better ability to actually hear what is being said, whether verbally or "between the lines". You can become better at not just focusing on the actual words that have been said and their literal meanings, instead you can be able to better understand the true meaning of the combined spoken words and what is not said. This will help build a fuller understanding of the feelings and emotions that the speaker is conveying on the subject.

When others are talking many of us are just using this time to formulate what we are going to say next, judging the speaker or waiting for the other person to say something that we disagree with. Often we approach conversations from the position of how it affects us when what we should be doing is trying to understand how it affects the speaker. When the speaker feels that they are being understood and not judged for what they are saying and expressing, they are more likely to open up and help strengthen the emotional connection between the speaker and the listener.

By being more attentive and listening with understanding, generosity, empathy, support, compassion, care and in a non judgemental way you can better understand what the speaker is trying to convey to you, including their feelings and emotions on a subject. Active listening also involves waiting for the other person to complete what they are saying fully before forming any opinion or starting to formulate a response if one is needed.

Before you can perfect your active listening techniques you need to use mindfulness to become more self aware, as until you truly understand and are friends with yourself you cannot be sure that what you are interpreting from other person's communication is not based upon your own misunderstanding of yourself. If you cannot fully understand the feelings and emotions of your own experiences you cannot appreciate those of others with any accuracy. Effectively you need to be able to use your own reliable experiences of feelings and emotions to be able to interpret and be empathetic to somebody else's.

Even when what is being said to us may sound like criticism or sound hurtful we can use mindfulness to show us that we can still care for ourselves while at the same time caring for the other person, and for what they are saying. Mindfulness teaches us to be here in this moment attentively with a knowing that it will be history very shortly, along with all the feelings and emotions that are attached to what is being said. By not reacting and actively listening to everything that is being said before you consider a response, you can often move past your initial negative reactive feelings and emotions to more positive ones as you realise that with better understanding comes a better perception of the other person's point of view.

We all want to be better understood, especially by the

people we care about most. A better understanding and appreciation of the other person's point of view will lead to a more attentive, compassionate and empathetic response. This will only improve the speaker's feelings of being understood. This will likely help them express more openly and more often, only helping you to understand and appreciate them furthermore. Active listening takes a conscious effort, time and practice but with usually quick and noticeable results. This is a technique many more of us should learn to perfect.

A good rule of thumb is to listen for twice as long as you speak, and the quality of your listening should be considered as important as the quality of your argument. Your argument or position will be stronger if it is formed upon a more solid understanding and appreciation of the other side because you have listened well. Often this will lead to agreement as many disagreements come from just miscommunication, either through what is said not being clear or from what is heard incorrectly. There are many techniques and names for active listening along with many meditations that will help you improve these skills and also help enhance your self awareness too.

With better understanding and appreciation you will

become better at providing support and care to the people you care about. This will serve everyone involved and relationship well.

Become Less Reactive

Regardless of the type of relationship, no two people can agree on everything all of the time. Sometimes we disagree so strongly that it can lead to an argument often caused by instinctive reactions that are triggered by what is being said by the other. We can all remember a time where we have reacted instinctively to something being said that we perceive as hurtful or wrong. In almost all cases reacting instinctively does not serve your ultimate aim which is resolve the argument as quickly as possible in the most amicable way. So by using mindfulness to notice negative emotions bubbling you can teach yourself to respond thoughtfully instead of instinctively reacting.

Instinctive reactions are not controlled actions, they are by their nature actions without thought and stem from your natural instinct to protect yourself. The problem with this natural instinct is that it evolved to protect us from getting eaten by bears when we lived in caves and not for living the lives and relationships we have now. This is why we find ourselves saying things we wouldn't normally say and regretting them later.

An instinctive reaction is an action that is not controlled so you are effectively out of control when you just react. Feeling out of control not only doesn't feel very nice for ourselves, it often makes the other person feel pretty bad too through what is done or said. So anything that reduces this type of behaviour can only benefit a relationship.

By practising mindfulness regularly you will learn how to intercept the reaction before it happens or at the very least while it's happening so you can pause and compose yourself, so that you can respond in a more thoughtful manner. Just the act of practising mindfulness regularly will help when going into situations where you disagree with another as your starting point emotionally is generally more balanced and centred. You will also be more aware of your emotions and feelings generally, so you will likely be able to raise issues or concerns long before they are likely to result in instinctive and intense reactions.

Relationships test us in many ways, especially emotionally. Mindfulness will not stop you feeling the emotions and feelings that come and go as a result of a particular relationship and it's interactions. However, being more mindful will help you better understand what you are feeling and help you to react less, and potentially do less damage to a relationship that is important to you. You will likely also become more proactive when it comes to discussing issues and concerns about how you feel, before they become major problems that can trigger arguments.

A more mindful you will also better understand the other's emotional state and other factors that may be influencing what they are saying that may hurt your feelings. By having this better understanding and empathy for the other person in this relationship, you will be less likely to react instinctively and make better decisions for the good of the relationship. Even if you do get caught out and do react instinctively, a more mindful you will help you recover to a more composed state quicker and with a stronger understanding of how the instinctive reaction will impact and affect the other along with the relationship.

Improved Emotional Intelligence

Good or bad relationships are generally built on how well you can affect the other person's feelings and emotions in a positive or a negative manner. By increasing your emotional intelligence you can improve a relationship by having a better understanding of how what you say and do affects someone else. Likewise with improved emotional intelligence you will be able to better understand how someone else's actions and comments affect you emotionally.

The act of practising mindfulness causes you to think about and examine how you feel in the present moment. This increased awareness of yourself, your own feelings and emotions can only help improve your relationships with others. Having an increased awareness of your own feelings will also help you better understand the other person, their feelings and emotions in the relationship too.

Emotional intelligence can be learned like many other skills, it just takes some effort but the rewards will be felt across your live in so many positive ways. Many are now saying that emotional intelligence is as, or even more important than intellectual intelligence. With greater emotional intelligence you will likely see your relationships with everyone improve, affecting your romantic life, your family life, your work life and your social life.

Improving your emotional intelligence through regular practice of mindfulness will not only help you become more self aware of how you feel, but will also help you relate and empathise with how others feel too. An improved self awareness will likely lead to you being better able to communicate your feelings and emotions sooner and before they potentially become an issue in the relationship. An improved general awareness of others feelings and emotions will also allow you to change your behaviour, actions and / or compromise sooner, hopefully before becoming an issue in the relationship.

With an overall better awareness of feelings and emotions and how they affect you and others, will improve how everyone in the relationship feels about being more open and vulnerable. Improved emotional intelligence through mindfulness practice will help you listen more and have a greater degree of understanding of how someone is receiving what you are saying. Improved emotional intelligence will likely lead to more emotional intimacy, which strengthens relationships.

Show More Empathy

There are several types of empathy but in terms of relationships, emotional empathy is probably the most important. Emotional empathy is the ability to feel as someone else does by picking up the non-verbal signs, verbal information and body language. Everyone in a relationship likes to feel they are understood and this is an important factor in strengthening the bonds between people. When you feel understood in a relationship you feel that the relationship is more fulfilling and in turn open up for more understanding and become more invested in that relationship.

Mindfulness has been shown to increase empathy in those who practice it regularly. By improving your awareness of the present moment on many fronts including how you feel gives you a greater understanding of how others are feeling too, making you more empathetic to them. Your communication with another person becomes more empathetic as you understand their internal world better and with compassion. Many experts believe that empathy is a fundamental component of all relationships in one form or another.

By being more empathetic and understanding of your partner in a relationship you are conveying not only that you care, you are also improving the connection and trust that you have with them.

Experience Less Stress

Stress can be caused by any number of issues from work to health problems but it can seriously impact your relationships in a negative way. Often the cause of the stress is from outside of the relationship and has the effect of pushing you further apart within the relationship. Stress also has another side effect, when we are stressed, for whatever reason, we feel less secure in our relationships as a result.

Stress can make us more irritable and less tolerant of small things that wouldn't normally worry us. Stress has an impact on our communication skills making us less able to converse in a positive manner. Stress also negatively affects how you perceive your relationship with another. Also stress and anxiety have been shown to make us attracted to other people instead of focusing on the one we're already with. Stress even when caused by life and experiences outside of the relationship can mark the end of the relationship unless accepted and brought under control.

Regular mindfulness practice helps reduce your stress levels by helping you become more balanced and centred. By being less stressed you will be less likely to overreact, less likely to be irritable, more tolerant and positive about all aspects of your life including the relationship. With consistent mindfulness practice you are aiming to approach stressful situations more as a challenge instead of a threat. Stress adds up, the more stressful you tend to feel, the more stressful another event or situation then feels, adding to the stressed and anxious feelings you already have.

It only needs one of you in the relationship to start suffering with stress at work or somewhere else for it to start to cause issues within the relationship. If you are more irritable and less tolerant of your partner, they are likely to start mirroring that behaviour or change their behaviour to avoid conflict as well potentially start to develop feelings of resentment.

Likewise though, with just one of you practising mindfulness each day, the benefits will be felt by both too. As the person suffering with the stress starts to feel the benefits of mindfulness and feeling less stressful and anxious, their partner will relax more too. Even if the person practising mindfulness is not the one currently suffering with the stress, they will be more empathetic, more compassionate and more tolerant of the others stress related behaviour and will also likely help reduce the stress levels of their partner.

Become More Accepting

Many of us may not be happy to accept that we all have our flaws, some more than others, but we all have them whether we like them or not. No person on this planet is perfect and perfection cannot be achieved however hard you try.

Acceptance is a fundamental principle of mindfulness practice. Part of being mindful is accepting how you feel in the present moment, whether that be pain, emotions or feelings. Being mindful will also help you accept what your flaws are and enable you to be more conscious of them when interacting with people, hopefully making your communications and interactions happier and more positive. Once you have accepted that you are not perfect and have flaws then you have to accept that everyone else has flaws too. When you accept that the other person in your relationship has flaws as well and assuming you are prepared to accept those flaws as part of that person, you will become less irritated by them.

Mindfulness also teaches us to accept situations as they are are in the moment too. Often our natural reaction to painful and distressing situations is to avoid them and not acknowledge what we are feeling in the moment. But by not fully accepting what is being experienced right now, we are just putting off having to deal with these feelings and either prolong the pain or suppress them to be dealt with later. In both these cases it is almost always likely to mean that more suffering is involved over a prolonged period and often without a resolution to the cause.

If you are more mindful and accept a situation for what it is, along with how it feels with all the pain and hurt that it may bring, you are then better placed to start making the changes to stop it occurring again. If you have not fully accepted what it is you are feeling, you cannot know for sure that any changes that you do make will make the right differences or cause you additional suffering. Acceptance is not about changing how you feel but accepting everything that you do feel and experience in the moment. The acceptance will likely be the first step in a chain reaction that helps rectify the cause too.

Build Stronger Relationships

Mindfulness helps develop a better sense of self awareness of the thoughts and feelings that you are having and it teaches you to respond deliberately, non judgmentally and with compassion to oneself. This provides you with better self-esteem, inner confidence and independence. All of these traits when brought to a relationship will help you be stronger in the relationship as well help strengthen the relationship itself.

Your general well-being will improve with mindfulness

including self-acceptance, self-compassion and give you a fuller understanding of your purpose in life. This will help improve the quality of any relationship especially if both parties are in a similar state of well-being. The sense of self that mindfulness brings will enable you to pursue personal and relationship goals with an authenticity in line with your true values and beliefs.

7

BEING HAPPIER AT WORK

JUST BELIEVE IN YOURSELF.
EVEN IF YOU DON'T, PRETEND
THAT YOU DO AND AT SOME
POINT YOU WILL.
VENUS WILLIAMS

The busy world we all work in now requires us to flip flop our attention from the actual work and functions we are paid to do and to responding to emails, taking telephone calls, making presentations and attending meetings to name just a few distractions. I'm sure you're already thinking there is enough on your plate at work to distract from completing your tasks without adding in mindfulness too. However, by being more mindful at work you will quickly learn that you can become more productive and happier doing your job.

Many large corporations are starting to realise that by encouraging staff to incorporate mindfulness into their lives that they will not only see the benefits in the workplace and improvements to their bottom line, but their staff are generally happier with life too. Even if you don't work in a large corporation that offers mindfulness sessions and meditations to its staff you can easily see the benefits yourself by taking the step of practising mindfulness on your own. You will likely become more productive, enjoy work more and it could be the next step towards your career goals.

Improve Your Attention

Being able to give your full attention to a task or a goal at work is fundamental to completing or achieving it in a timely and productive manner. Many of us including our employers underestimate just how important attention is to the job at hand really is to staff performance, productivity and their happiness in the workplace. With each year that passes, technology increases in speed or there is another tool or distraction created that draws attention away from the job you are actually paid to do. Effectively your attention becomes divided, giving you less time and sporadic focus on the main roles of your job. Being able to focus and maintain your attention on a particular task becomes more difficult and more important with more distractions. Focused attention is a skill that can be programmed into the mind and once learnt will help in many areas of life, not just work.

Being mindful requires us to focus on the here and now by being in the present moment instead of just allowing our minds to wander with no form of monitoring. Effectively it's a form of attention focus and to be able to complete your tasks effectively and with fewer errors that you need to be focused on the task at hand. Contrary to popular belief, human minds are not capable of multitasking, they are only capable of single tasking or thinking of one thing at a time. What human brains are good at is jumping from one thought to another so quickly that it seems like multitasking. This means you are not fully focusing your attention on just one thing while this is happening and this is where mindfulness comes in.

Typically to start with, mindfulness teaches you to focus on your breath only, this trains your mind to maintain focus in the present moment, on your breath. It also teaches you that when your mind does wander that this is okay, but attention needs to be brought back to your breathing again, making you refocus your attention. Studies show that this action of focusing on your breath and re-focusing when the mind wanders trains your brain and effectively creates a process that can be applied for focusing on other things too.

By practising mindfulness consistently you will notice that at work when you have a specific task to complete and you are being distracted by emails, telephone calls, social media and colleagues, you will find refocusing easier, saving you time and errors. Ideally mindfulness will show you that you can maintain focus on the task at hand even while other distractions occur, by acknowledging their occurrence and accepting that they will be dealt with after your task is complete.

A simple exercise to help train your mind for better attention, is at the start of the working day or in a break, set the timer on you mobile phone for a minute and in that minute focus only on your breathing. Notice the breath coming in through your nostrils, the air moving down into your lungs and effect on your body as the air is exhaled through your mouth. If your mind wanders, this is fine and don't criticise yourself, just bring your attention back to your breathing again.

As you become more proficient at maintaining your focus you will also start to be able to control where your focus is placed. You will be able to consciously move attention from one task to another as you choose instead of reacting to the latest call on your attention. This will not only benefit you at work but will also help in all areas of your life and help you understand how important attention and focus are for whatever you are trying to achieve in life.

Improve Your Performance

There are several factors that affect your performance at work including relationships with colleagues, customers and suppliers, your overall well-being, how you respond to criticism, your general communication skills, your ability to lead others and how you respond to stress. These are just a few but by improving these through mindfulness will almost definitely lead to improvements in your performance at work.

Mindfulness helps you develop compassion, self awareness and emotional regulation. By improving these traits it will help you develop a better understanding of yourself and those around you which is fundamental to building and maintaining relationships whether at work or in life generally. Someone that has these traits and can cultivate relationships in a caring and understanding manner is an asset to any team.

By practising mindfulness on a regular basis you will likely improve your general well-being which usually comes with several performance enhancing attributes. With a better general well-being you are likely to be more confident and more sure in your own abilities and offer yourself less doubt. You are also likely to understand where your current limitations extend enabling you to know when you should ask for assistance or advice.

You are also likely to just be generally calmer, helping you deal with comments and criticisms from others with a more constructive approach. Mindfulness helps you to be less judgmental of others which will help you to understand whether criticism is valid or whether it should be dismissed.

A key element to mindfulness is to listen to yourself whether that be emotionally, physically or psychologically. Using this skill when listening to others along with just listening more, will help build relationships with colleagues, customers and suppliers. It will also help you learn more and what you learn could be fundamental to completion of a task in a quicker or improved manner. Taking a bit more time to listen to what others in the workplace have to say could lead to massive improvements in your performance.

If you are a manager or leader of others in the workplace they are more likely to respond and perform if you are calm, decisive and self regulated. By improving your own performance at work you can also improve the performance or others around you or beneath you, just by association. Often performance is a team effort and how you behave and act can have a direct impact on others and that also has a knock on effect to the team's overall performance too.

Improve Your Stress Management

Stress in the workplace nowadays is an all too common phenomenon that affects almost all of us at some point. Stress from work seems to be increasing, working hours are being lost and it is damaging workers health mentally and in some instances psychically too. While many employers are aware and keen to help employees reduce stress from work, it is important to take control of your own stress and anxiety regardless of what your employer may offer. Stress regardless of its source affects every area of your life. Learning how to cope and deal with stress induced from work is key if it is not going to affect your performance, and your personal life too.

By reducing your work related stress you should expect to see improvements in absenteeism through sickness, increased job satisfaction, higher levels of motivation, increased attention, better decision making, more creativity and better relationship skills with colleagues. You owe it to yourself and your life to understand your own stress and do whatever you must do to reduce it. With improved understanding and control over your work related stress you could potentially further your career and have more successes, not just at work but throughout your life.

One of the most important factors when dealing with stress is recognising that you are starting to feel anxious and stressful about a situation, a deadline, a goal or similar. Mindfulness helps with this by encouraging you to be more aware of your feelings and emotions in the present moment. Once you have the skills to notice how your emotions and feelings are changing, you can make other changes to help cope or reduce these feelings.

As regular mindfulness practice helps calm your mind allowing you to see things with greater clarity it should reduce the impact of stressful situations which should help you make better and more confident decisions. This is not to say you won't suffer with stress, as we all do at some point but mindfulness teaches us that it is a feeling that will pass in time if we accept it without giving it too much focus. Mindfulness also teaches us that stress and anxiety are often rooted and multiplied in our own thoughts and that they are just that, only thoughts. Many stressful and anxious feelings rise from perception instead of the reality of the situation.

Mindfulness helps you understand your own personal relationship with stress, what triggers your stressful feelings and what causes them to increase. Mindfulness also encourages compassion and empathy for yourself as well as others at work. As you practice mindfulness, the way you approach life including work will change helping you to become less prone to stress but there are many small mindfulness techniques that you can practice at work when you are starting to notice the stressful feelings bubble up.

Improve Your Emotional Control

While many companies like to think that emotions should be left at home, this is just not possible although you can learn how to manage and regulate your emotions using mindfulness. In the workplace as with anywhere else in life, emotions play a role in how well you perform, your stress levels, your productivity, your relationships and decision making. So if you want to be more productive, perform better, manage your stress levels and improve your work relationships then learning how to regulate your emotions is important. You should not underestimate how important your emotions are or those of your employees.

Without control and conscious effort, when an emotion arises we react instinctively which can have all sorts of effects on those we work with, what we think of ourselves in the workplace and can slow down your career progression. Instead of reacting, mindfulness teaches us to pause when we have the urge to react and instead make a considered response if one is needed. A considered response when others would react will help how you are perceived by your colleagues and managers and could help improve your career progress too.

There are many studies that show that mindfulness helps with emotional regulation and lessens emotional reactivity. Mindfulness encourages you to accept what emotions that you are feeling with compassion and curiosity. Studies are also showing that the more you practice mindfulness, the less you have to actively manage your emotions, as it becomes a subconscious skill.

There are several proactive techniques you can implement easily to help manage your emotions at work. Firstly make sure you use the awareness that mindfulness brings to notice when emotions start to bubble up as early as possible, so you are prepared for the likely reactions to watch out for and start preparing yourself to pause and respond when and if needed. You can also think about situations or tasks that cause specific problem emotions in you and either avoid them or plan for them well enough in advance and take as much control as is possible.

For situations that cannot be avoided or adjusted to make them less emotionally charged for you, use your mindfulness skills to focus your attention on what it is you should be doing instead of the emotions themselves. Mindfully accept that the emotions are there and that they will pass shortly unless you start to focus your attention on them. While it may be tempting to suppress any emotions you are experiencing and it may work for you in the short term, suppressed emotions will come out later and usually with greater impact.

Improve Your Decision Making

We all have to make some form of decisions at work. The higher you are in an organisation the wider the potential implications of the decisions you make. Sometimes we do not fully appreciate the full implications of our decision making at work until something goes wrong. By becoming more mindful about the decisions you take at work you can increase your confidence and the confidence of others in your decision making, which can only help your career.

As most of us know the difference between right and wrong, we know what is expected of us as an employee and what the main goals of the business are. We should be able to make our decisions that support all of these criteria. However, sometimes it's not always clear which decision best serves us, our role and/or the business. Sometimes there may be perceived conflicts or the decision that needs to be taken may make us feel uncomfortable.

Mindfulness teaches us to be present and to have an openness to whatever we feel about a particular decision. It teaches us to view how we feel with compassion, empathy and curiosity so you can consider, how each decision will affect how you feel and how it may affect others, or the business overall. By being more aware and attentive to decisions before you make them, you should be able to make decisions without allowing your ego and self judgement to influence and in the best interests of you, your role and business.

While you are using mindfulness to make a more considered approach to decisions you should notice that there are less mistakes compared to knee jerk reaction based decisions. You should also find that decisions are a lot less emotionally based making them more likely to be correct.

8

HOW TO BE MINDFUL

MINDFULNESS IS A WAY
OF BEFRIENDING OURSELVES
AND OUR EXPERIENCE
JON KABAT-ZINN

Mindfulness is very simply the act of paying attention to what is going on right now in the present moment whether that be inside or outside of your body and your mind.

Mindfulness is about living in the present moment and not ruminating on what has happened in the past or worrying about what is going to happen in the future. What has happened in the past cannot be changed and what is going to happen in the future is purely in your imagination in the present moment. The present moment is the only time that you can actually affect your life by making decisions, it is the only time you can experience life as it happens to you and it is the only time you can affect your future.

By being more in the present moment you will find that life is more enjoyable, happier and fuller as you will be experiencing more of it. There are some fundamental principles to mindfulness that you should always bear in mind when practising.

Be Present

The most important element of mindfulness is being present now. There are several ways you can do this but just being aware that you should be in the present moment more often is a good start, as most us don't think about time and life this way. The most obvious ways of making sure you are in the present moment are:

- **Notice how you feel** When you catch yourself thinking about something that happened in the past or worrying about something in the future take notice of how it is making you feel right now in the present.

  Remind yourself that these are just thoughts and not what is happening to you right now. Choose to focus on what is happening around you right now and try to notice visually and audibly what is going on and how you feel about it.

- **Do just one thing at a time** We are used to having to juggle multiple tasks most of the time. It's especially more difficult with mobile phones around us all the time, pinging and buzzing trying to get our attention.

  Choose to focus on one task and ignore all other calls on you attention for a while. Set yourself a time limit if it is easier. If you are pouring a glass of water, only pour a glass of water and don't think about anything else other than pouring the glass of water. If you are cleaning the bathroom, only think about the action of cleaning and all that it involves with sights, smells and sounds.

By focusing on the only thing you are doing in the present moment you will enjoy it more, be better at it and likely complete your task quicker and you would have been present throughout.

- **Take your time** By acting slowly and deliberately you will notice more of the present moment naturally. Think about each action before you take it regardless of how small or trivial it may seem. Ask yourself why are you doing whatever it is you are doing this way.

  As you take actions notice the effects on the present moment. It could be a change in how you feel, what you see, smell, hear or sense through touch. By taking your time you allow yourself time to notice more of what is happening now.

- **Schedule Space** When you make plans or plan

your day make sure you allow yourself time in between tasks or events to slow down and notice what is going on in the present. We all too often schedule tasks, events or appointments back to back and don't allow ourselves some "breathing" space in between to recentre and balance ourselves again before the next item on our agenda.

In these gaps take the opportunity to notice what has changed in the way you feel since the last time you checked. Spend a moment with yourself or take a break and go for a quick walk. Just spend some time with yourself, your feelings and your senses for a moment.

- **Pay Attention** Whether it's when someone is talking to you or whether you are out and about on your own, just pay attention without allowing your mind to wander off. We all do it when someone is talking to us, we start thinking about our response before they've even finished what they are saying or our minds are somewhere completely different altogether.

Try just listening to what is being said right

now and wait to form any opinions until they have completely finished talking. When you are out and about pay attention to what you are seeing now and not what you already know is there. The same goes for listening as well as for your other senses. You will be surprised how much you miss when you're not actively paying attention.

- **Eat Slower** Mindful eating is a far broader subject than just eating more slowly but just the act of consciously slowing down your eating brings you into the present moment. By eating more slowly you will enjoy your food a lot more, enjoy the company more and find the whole experience more enjoyable. Take a few more chews of your mouthful, put your cutlery down between bites and join in with conversation with the other people you are eating with.

After all, you or someone you care about is paying for what you are eating, maybe they have prepared it for you too and even if you are eating alone, by taking time to savour your food it will help you remain in the present moment. You are also less likely to overeat as it gives your brain a chance to keep up with what is going inside you.

There are many ways in which you can help yourself be more present. The more you do it, the more you notice more ways it can be done.

Be Open

By being more open to experiencing everything that you feel and what others think and feel will enrich your life further. By being more open you will discover that other people will also respond with more openness and you will learn more about yourself and others too. In the cynical world we live, being open can be perceived as a sign of weakness or can make you feel vulnerable. However, openness with oneself comes with a better understanding of why you may feel this way and how that it is related to your own ego and how you believe others may perceive you.

- **Being Open with Yourself** Many of us are not open with ourselves about how we are feeling in any given moment for many reasons. A common reason is for emotional self protection so we don't have to experience negative feelings as we are having them through fear of how we will react. However by not acknowledging what you are feeling in the moment you are storing up those feelings to manifest themselves later and often in way that is unexpected.

As you learn to be more open with yourself about how you are feeling in the present, you will start to learn that feelings come and go all the time and if allowed they will generally pass without incident. You will learn that you can prolong a feeling by focusing on it more and if left alone it will change to another feeling relatively quickly on it's own.

To start with, being open with yourself about exactly what you are feeling can make you feel vulnerable, as it feels like you will have less control of yourself. However you are just changing what you are controlling. By experiencing what you are really feeling in the present doesn't mean you lose control, instead your control is now based upon a better and well informed you.

You will learn that how you feel in any moment is your feeling and no one else's. Others may induce feelings in you but they are your feelings and you should understand them and their context in the present moment.

- **Being Open with Others** Obviously how open you are with others is a judgement about that particular relationship but generally the more open you are, the more it will improve the relationship. In fact, if you make a decision to open up or not open up, you can mindfully ask yourself why you are coming to this decision.

Once you have understood how to be open with yourself, you can then become more open with others as you will understand yourself better and can convey exactly how you feel with honesty. Nobody can argue or tell you that what you feel is wrong, as how you feel is how you feel. They may not understand why you feel the way you do but by using your openness towards yourself you hopefully will understand your feelings better, and be able to explain what has caused you to feel the way you do.

Being open about how you feel with other people will help them feel more comfortable with being more open with you, along with helping build trust between each other. At first the act of sharing how you feel can make you feel that you are exposed emotionally, but the more you do it the easier it becomes. You will usually find that people respond with kindness, understanding or at least an attempt at understanding.

Do not be disheartened if understanding of how you feel is not forthcoming as this is usually a reflection of the others insecurities around trust, lack of understanding of their own feelings or just disinterest. Openness about how you feel with others can only help improve your interactions with people and relationships you have that are important to you.

- **Being Open Towards Others** Once you have opened up and shared your feelings with someone else it makes it a lot easier for them to explain about their feelings too. Once you are more open about your own feelings it is a lot easier to understand someone else when they explain theirs.

Just by you opening up you can create an environment that enables both parties to express their feelings more. That's not to say the other person will or it may take them some time but by being more open yourself you are enabling it to happen. When someone else opens up about how they feel, give them the same understanding that you would give yourself when it comes to your feelings.

Remember to be present and listen instead of just waiting to speak. You may not understand why they feel a certain way but with a better understanding of your own feelings, at least you might be able understand what it is that they are feeling. This is a form of empathy. When someone feels they are being understood they are more likely to open up further.

Being more open with yourself, others and empathising more with others about their feelings could well open doors to a world you didn't know existed before, and a much more meaningful and fulfilling life.

Be Non Judgemental

We judge each other either in good or bad ways and in

so many different ways without even realising we are doing it most of the time. More importantly we are harsher judges of ourselves than of others. We are all trying to measure ourselves or others against images, stereotypes, egos, etc. and forming judgments upon these measurements, either correctly or incorrectly. What might be a correct judgement of someone today may not reflect a correct judgement of them as a whole. Likewise we can easily judge ourselves incorrectly too. Often our judgements are based upon our past and experiences which may have no bearing or relevance on who we are judging now.

The society that we live in is competitive by nature and while most aspire for something better, it is all too easy to be influenced by so many different factors. The only real solution is to practice being less judgmental as much as possible. We need to notice when we have made a judgement of ourself or another and potentially suspend that judgement indefinitely, or until we have more information.

The reason we usually judge someone, something or ourselves is down to how we feel about it or them at the time of making the judgement. The problem is that often once judgements are made it's difficult to overturn them in our minds. If you take some time to understand how you are feeling in the present it may help you understand where your judgement is coming from and whether it is fair. Are you judging them or yourself based upon what someone else said or did to make you feel this way in the past? Are you judging them without all the facts or information? Are you judging yourself based upon unrealistic media portrayals. Some ways to judge less:

- **First Impressions Don't Count** There is a lot to be said for making a good first impression however we all have off days and would you like to be judged by someone else based upon how you are on an off day? We all come in different shapes, sizes, colours, orientations and personalities. If you base all your decisions on people on their first impressions, your life could be something completely different to what it is now.

  If someone makes a bad first impression, give them a break in the same way that you hope you would get a break on a bad day from other people. They probably know that they're having a bad day, so by you not passing instant judgement on them could help improve their day too.

Likewise if someone makes a good first impression, all may not be what it seems initially. It takes time to get to know people and often your opinion of many people will change over time too.

Should you really make a judgement on someone before you've got to know them? 'Obviously no' you are probably thinking but we all do it whether we admit it or not. Being mindful would mean that you notice when you're making or have made a judgement and choosing to suspend judgement until you've got to know someone for a while.

- **Compare less** When we make a judgment it is almost always based upon a comparison to something or someone else. Often these comparisons are either ill-informed or based more upon our own ego and insecurities we have about ourselves than anything in reality. Simply by making less comparisons we will judge less.

It is the same when you judge that someone is good or bad, tall or short, fat or slim, nice or nasty and so on. The same applies when we judge ourselves too, we are comparing ourselves to other people or what we believe others are or how they would act or feel.

- **Forget roles** When you make a judgment on someone, your role in relation to them should make no difference to the judgement of them. Whether you are a parent, spouse, partner, child, friend, boss, employee, etc. it should not cloud how you judge someone.

Your judgements should be based purely on the other person, their personality, actions and words. Basing judgements upon your role in relation to them doesn't take into account the rest of their life and who they really are. Likewise by dropping your roles, you allow yourself to be who you really are instead of the roles you've been assigned by society, yourself and others.

- **Value All Ages** With age comes wisdom and with youth comes exuberance and naivety. We all have heard that we should respect our elders but we should also respect our youngsters too. Making judgements based upon age can be a huge mistake for many reasons.

Someone who is older often has the benefit of experience and past mistakes that often many can learn from. On the flip side, being older can mean that you are less willing to try new things and are slower to accept change. Someone who is younger may not have the benefit of experience but has the enthusiasm for trying new things and embracing change.

Obviously just because you are young does not mean you do not have experiences that many of us can learn from too. As is the case with older people, they are not likely to be wise on all subjects. Ultimately we all have something to offer each other if we aren't quick to judge and allow each other time and space in a non judgemental way to demonstrate what we have to offer and are capable of.

- **Know You** You are unique in so many ways and it is something you should celebrate. What makes us unique is everything that makes us wonderfully different from any other person, including all our life experiences whether good or bad. The more you are aware of how you feel about yourself, the less likely you are to be judgmental and critical of others. If you have a better understanding of what it is to be you with all your abilities and flaws, you are less likely to judge others for theirs so quickly.

Do not try to change yourself to please others, make people like you or to conform to other peoples ideas. You will lose your character and personality that makes you uniquely you. Just by being yourself and understanding yourself, will attract the right people into your life. Ensure that you are present as much as possible to understand how things make you feel and listening to the signals that your body provides so you can make the right choices for you in your life.

• **Embrace diversity** As mentioned above we all are unique and come in varying colours, beliefs, orientations and natural tongues. Someone being different to you should be treated as an opportunity to learn instead of judgement. If we all looked the same and had the same beliefs it would be a very uninteresting world. Instead of assuming you already know or ignorantly not being interested, take the chance to widen your knowledge and horizons and learn as much as you can from other people.

Taking the opportunity to learn from others regardless of their backgrounds and appearance will only increase your own knowledge and abilities to interact with more people. In the same way you expect others to listen to you and your opinions without judgement, you should be present enough to ensure you do the same for others regardless of who they are.

By being less judgmental you open up the possibilities to learn more and create stronger and more meaningful relationships. If you leap to judge too early you could be restricting yourself now and in the future in all sorts of ways.

Be Accepting

Having more acceptance for what something or a situation really is will help you respond in the correct manner, instead of either responding inappropriately or not at all. If you do not accept things for the way they are and instead fight it, you are wasting energy on denying the truth when you could be spending that energy on improving the situation. So by accepting things as they are, in truth you might have to face some harsh realities, but you will be better placed to move forward too. You need to be accepting of yourself, others and situations for what they really are. If you are kidding yourself about something you are creating your own obstacles. Ways to be more accepting:

- **Be positive** Often why we don't accept others, ourselves or situations is because we have noticed a negative or something we don't like. As mentioned before, we all have our faults but most of us have many positive traits. Accept that not everyone including yourself can be perfect and focus on their or your positive qualities more.

Lost some money?
Remember that you could have lost a friend.

Lost your job?
You could have lost your sight.

Lost your home?
You could have lost a child.

Things don't always go as planned but accept, acknowledge and appreciate what you still have more often. When we accept ourselves, people and situations for what they really are, warts and all, they become far less daunting, often more interesting propositions and sometimes new opportunities. When you are more accepting of people, you will often find that they are more accepting of you too. So try to notice the positive in everyone and everything where you can and you will find it a lot easier to accept them.

- **Think in greys** It is very easy for us to think of the world as black and white or as right and wrong. However the world is very rarely like this in reality. Usually something or someone is partly right and often partly wrong at the same time. By taking the view that someone or something can only be either wholly right or wrong causes you an issue, as most things are a bit of both. Which side do you come down on? If you do come down on one side, now you are partly right and partly wrong.

Once you are more accepting that there is more to the world than viewing it in just black and white and accept all the various shades of grey in between. You will start to experience the world in a new way and people will become more accepting of you and your shades of grey too. When you are present, take note if you start to think in this black and white manner and try to see if there are any greys.

- **Pay attention to thoughts** While you are in the present moment, notice whether your thoughts are rushing you to form an opinion of someone or something without considering all the facts or information. It is only when you consider all the information that you have, can you accept things for how they really are. Our mind is very good at tricking us into noticing negative things and giving them higher value than positive things.

  You should be suspicious of your mind if you can only notice negative or just positive thoughts relating to someone or something. There are exceptions obviously but almost everything has pros and cons and make sure your mind is presenting them all to you so you can accept things as they are, instead of what your mind wants you to think.

- **About turn** One good technique is to turn the tables. Imagine if someone else was judging you and not accepting you for the thoughts and beliefs that you have of someone else, instead of the reality of how things actually are. Would it be fair? Would you like it? Obviously not, so why treat someone else in a way that you would not like to be treated.

Likewise, you apply this to accepting yourself more too. Accept yourself for who you really are too. We all make mistakes and say the wrong things and things that we don't mean at times, accept that this is normal human behaviour. If you can accept someone else is human with faults, you must treat yourself no differently.

Be Connected

Part of mindfulness is connecting with ourselves and with the rest of the world to understand we are part of something bigger. By accepting who you are with all your faults and qualities will help you connect with yourself at a deeper level. Once you can connect with yourself in a truthful and open way you will find it easier to connect with others too. Ways you can connect with yourself and others:

- **Ask for help** Asking someone close to you about you can be empowering but also might make you feel vulnerable initially. Explain that you are trying to improve yourself by better understanding yourself. People that are close and care about you will often notice things about you that you don't, or just take for granted as normal. Assuming their comments are honest and truthful you have an opportunity to better understand yourself and potentially identify areas that you can improve on.

You may find some of their comments aren't what you were expecting or they may make you feel like they are being too critical. However, please remember that they care about you and wouldn't intentionally say something to hurt you. You are trying to better understand and connect to yourself and they are helping you, even if you don't like some of what you hear. Accept what you are told with an intention of better understanding yourself, connecting with yourself and improving yourself. Most other people just see these types of comments as criticisms and do not take them as opportunities to improve themselves.

- **Appreciate more** It is one of the simplest

things you can do, it's free and will give you a warm feeling inside every time you do it. Not only that, it will help connect with yourself and others too. You will better connect with yourself if you appreciate what talents and positive qualities you have. You can also appreciate what negative qualities you have too and how they impact your life. By appreciating these you can focus on improving or changing them through better understanding and appreciation of how they affect you and others.

By appreciating others and what they bring to your life and those around you, you will better be able to connect with them. Appreciate all the positives that someone brings into your life and what your life would be like without these qualities. Even if you are appreciating the negatives that they bring into your life, you can at least understand, can make decisions and communicate your observations in a connected way.

Appreciate everything else in the world. The air that you breath and the quality of it, after all it's what keeps you alive. Appreciate nature, including all the plants, trees, animals and birds that surround you as you make your way through life. As they come into your world, you enter theirs too, so we are ultimately connected with everything. Appreciate that the thoughts and actions that you have now, have an impact on others and the world around you in some way or another.

- **Sense more** For most of us the most obvious sense is sight. Take more time in the present to notice everything that you see. Your sight and brain is taking in everything and every little detail from every blade of grass to every leaf on every tree. Your brain is clever enough to subconsciously filter out all of this detail so you don't have information overload and go mad, but start to notice some of this detail more consciously. There is a lot to see when you really look and who knows what you will see and what effect it may have, plus you will certainly feel a bit more connected to it.

As you move around your ears are taking in a continuous stream of sound. It's your subconscious brain that applies filters so you can differentiate important sounds from just the background noise. However there is a lot to hear in the background noise if you actually try to listen, whether that be aeroplanes passing overhead, traffic noise, the whirring of pumps and fans of buildings that you pass or birds chirping in a distant tree, or the rustle of the leaves in the wind, maybe the wind itself. When you can take a moment to use your ears to hear what is really happening around you, you will feel more connected to your environment.

There is an advertisement on TV at the moment for an air freshener that talks about nose blindness. Your brain filters out environmental smells so it can focus attention on noticing and highlight smells that are not normally associated with the current environment. This is called sensory adaptation and smell is where we experience it the most. Studies have shown that the more you think about smells the more you notice them, so every chance you can, take a moment to notice all the smells and aromas you can around you right now. Over time you should connect more with the world around you using smell and help reduce your nose blindness.

One of the easiest ways to feel connected with the world around you is through touch. We take so many of the things in our world that we touch for granted, either through our hands or other parts of our body. Take a moment to notice how something actually feels when it is in your hand. Notice the texture, how it moves and temperature for starters. You feel touch all over your body so pay attention to how clothes feels against your skin, whether parts of your body are feeling different temperatures.

Taste is one sense that we notice regularly but again our brain is very good at changing what it is that we actually experience as taste. Many studies have shown that what we call taste is made of up from various other senses too like sight and hearing. When you are eating, close your eyes for a couple of seconds and think about what you can taste in your mouth. Just by shutting off one of your senses you may notice more or a slightly different taste to the food. Obviously you can put your fingers in your ears as well to shut off another sense but you might get some funny looks in restaurants.

A sense that many of us aren't familiar with is

the Vestibular sense. The vestibular sense detects movement, rotation and relationship to things like gravity. This is how you know that you are moving when you in a lift that has no visible signs of movement to your other senses. Likewise it tells you whether you are standing or lying down when your eyes are closed. Try to tune into these feelings from the vestibular sense more often and notice what it is telling you in the moment.

Finally one often overlooked sense is Proprioception. This sense is how you know where various parts of your body are in relation to the rest of your body. For example you can clap your hands with your eyes closed because of proprioception. It also helps you understand where your body and where parts of it are in relation to the space and world around you, so you can plan movements.

When you get the chance take a moment to notice how you are connected to the world around you by using proprioception to notice the pressure your bum makes when sitting on a chair and where the weight of it is felt. Where and why your hands are where they are in relation to the rest of you. Almost all of proprioception happens in the subconscious but by noticing what is being sensed you will feel more connected to the world outside of you.

Be More Compassionate

Compassion is an emotional state which is in the form of feeling the distress in connection with another person's suffering. Compassion is a completely natural state that is hardwired into mammals to help us survive by caring for others. It is born from the understanding that we all wish to be happy and none of us wish to suffer. It's recognition that we all share similar experiences and can relate to the suffering that others are going through. We all have some form of compassion but some more than others. The good news is that compassion can be developed, so here are some pointers:

- **Focus outwards** Most highly compassionate people focus on others feelings and thoughts from a point of common understanding and show empathy that allows them to connect with others easily.

- **You can't buy it** Money doesn't buy you

happiness and it certainly doesn't buy compassion either. In fact studies have shown that people with more money tend to have less compassion. So if you have done well then you should redouble your efforts on the compassion front.

- **Teach** Compassionate people have a habit of sharing their knowledge with and for others to benefit from. When you teach someone else, you are giving them knowledge that can empower themselves to improve their own lives. So share your knowledge with others to help them just for the sake of helping them.

- **Be mindful** Just the act of feeling compassion for another must mean you are in the present moment to understand how they are feeling. Likewise if you are not in the present moment you will not notice and will not know when to show some compassion.

- **Be grateful** At some point or another someone will have shown you compassion, so why not feel grateful for that act. The very act of feeling grateful makes us feel good about ourselves and makes feeling compassion for someone else a lot easier.

Be More Self Compassionate

As human beings we all suffer at some point for one thing or another. Being self compassionate is accepting of ourself with a kindness and understanding that suffering is a normal part of life that we all go through. Practising self compassion will improve your happiness, your optimism, your curiosity and your extroversion. Why many of us don't practice as much self compassion as we should is due to too much self criticism, self isolation and self absorption.

Increasing self compassion will help improve how you feel about yourself. As Kristin Neff PhD says in her book Self Compassion, we should stop judging and evaluating ourselves together. Stop labelling aspects of ourselves as "good" or "bad" and simply accept ourselves with an open heart and treat ourselves with the same kindness, care and compassion as we would a close friend.

9

MINDFULNESS WITHOUT MEDITATION

ALMOST EVERYTHING WILL WORK
AGAIN IF YOU UNPLUG IT FOR A
FEW MINUTES...
INCLUDING YOU.

ANNE LAMOTT

Practising mindfulness is a skill that can be learned and applied to your daily life to help improve how you feel about it, moment to moment. However, being mindful is not something that you will do continuously throughout the day, instead you will learn when to take a mindful approach to situations, events and feelings. It's a skill like most others, that with more practice comes more proficiency in it. By practising mindfulness you will learn to choose when to be mindful and when not to be. By practising mindfulness you are aiming to create a habitual framework in your mind, that replaces bad habits and bad mental patterns.

With the seemingly non-stop rise in mental health issues in our society, mental health should be considered equally important as physical health. We all know how important physical health and diet is to our quality and length of life. Yet if you go back fifty years it just wasn't known or fully understood by the general population. It has taken time for the general population to gradually become educated into taking more responsibility for their own physical health. There now seems to be a similar shift when it comes to mental health too. More and more people are starting to understand that what goes on inside their minds can be controlled and influenced in a similar way that we do with our physical bodies.

As with any skill that can be learned it takes practice. Any moment when you are being mindful is considered practice, so the more you practice, the better you will become at it. Using mindfulness meditation is a very good way of focusing your full attention onto practising being mindful. This is equivalent to taking your mind for a workout in the same way you would take your body to the gym. Mindfulness meditation is comparative to running on a treadmill, compared to the walking you do going about you daily life. Obviously any walking is better for your physical health than no walking at all, but is does not compare to running at the gym or track.

When you were born, you didn't know how to do anything yet in the years since, you have learned thousands of skills that you apply everyday without even considering most of them. Ideally being more mindful should be a skill that we learn at an early age, but it's never too late to learn a new skill. Especially one that will likely have such a profound effect on the rest of your life. If it makes it easier, compare it to learning a new sport or a new skill in a sport that you already take part in.

There are many simple ways to practice being mindful in your everyday life and the more you practice, the better you will feel about your everyday life too. To ensure that you practice mindfulness routinely, you need to make being mindful a habit. One of the easiest ways to form a habit is to attach it to another habit that you already have. You have hundreds of habits that you perform everyday from brushing your teeth in the morning to lying down in bed at night. By adding being mindful to just these two habits would make you automatically mindful twice a day. Twice more a day than you are now! Whatever habits you choose to attach your mindful moments to, make sure you attach them to the end of the existing habit. It has been shown in many studies that the easiest way to adopt new habits is to attach them to the end of existing habits.

There are many other boring tasks that we all have to do that become opportunities to practice being mindful. Boring tasks are usually the moments when your mind will start to wander, maybe about doing something more interesting afterwards or maybe ruminating about events or situations that have occurred in the past. By being mindful in these moments you get more practice at mindfulness while not living inside your mind for a while. You have to do these tasks anyway, so you may as well take the opportunity to improve your mindfulness skills. Hopefully you will make them a bit more interesting in the process and maybe in a way that you hadn't considered before.

Being mindful in these kind of situations should be kept relatively short. A mistake that many who newly come to mindfulness make is to try to be mindful all the time or to be mindful throughout a whole task. The shorter the action the easier your mind finds it to make it habitual. Obviously once the habit is formed you can start increasing the length of your mindful moments, but if you do not form the habits you will not continue to be mindful for a sustained period. Consider how many habits you've tried to break with new year's resolutions, it is not very easy to break a habit once formed. Once the habit is formed, you can reinforce it with more time later, so start small.

Another mistake many people make is to set their targets too high. If you come to anything new with the intention of doing it for the rest of your life, you will likely fail. Key is to set a realistic target that you can achieve without too much effort, but with some effort. For example, if your intention is to practice mindfulness for the rest of your life you will never hit your target. Instead if you start with an intention of practising mindfulness for a week, you will be able to hit your target and receive the good feelings of achieving a target relatively quickly. You can extend your targets as you hit each one making them progressively harder as time goes by, but by making sure you can realistically achieve the next target you will be more likely to continue. You obviously know that your ultimate intention is be mindful forever, but by setting targets along the way that you can achieve you will make it more likely that you stick with it and achieve the ultimate target.

Being mindful throughout the day is easy once you have set yourself the intention to do it. Even if you decide to practice mindfulness meditation, being mindful more often throughout the day is the ultimate intention of all the practice. So how is this done? In any given moment being mindful is just using your senses to notice what is going on around you and noticing what you are experiencing internally with your feelings and emotions.

While you are being mindful in this way you cannot be thinking of something that happened earlier or worrying about what will happen later. It gives your mind a rest from worry and stress and trains you to focus your attention where you choose, instead of allowing your mind to choose for you. Your mind automatically filters out lots of information about the present moment that your senses are picking up all of the time. This is usually because your mind has decided it's not important to complete the current task or it is just taking in enough to keep you from harm while you ruminate or worry about something else. Part of being mindful is paying more attention to what your senses are detecting in the present moment and acknowledging them.

Mindfully Drinking Tea Or Coffee

Practising mindfulness can be done at any time and there are always opportunities throughout your day when just being a bit more mindful contributes to your overall well-being. Your first cup of coffee or tea after you wake up in the morning is a good place to start, or alternatively the first cup of coffee at work. Any drink and any time are opportunities but try to pick one drink that you have everyday so you can start making it part of the ritual of having the drink and forming a habit.

Start by setting an intention to focus on this next tea or coffee for a few minutes. Make your drink and find a quiet place to sit whether this is at the breakfast table or at your desk at work. Now focus on the cup and notice its shape, colour and size along with where it is sitting in your current world. Notice the colour of the drink itself as it cools. If steam is rising from the cup take a few moments to watch it dissipate above the cup.

When it is cool enough to drink, take a sip and feel the warmth on your lips and then your throat as it slides down. Notice the taste of the particular blend and how this drink makes you feel as you take each sip. If your mind wanders or gets distracted, bring it back to how the drink tastes and how much you are enjoying it.

Do not rush your drink and make sure you savour it. As it cools further notice the difference in temperature with each sip. Try to stay focused on the drink until it is finished, and when you have finished, take a moment to feel gratitude and appreciation of the drink and how good it feels to be able to enjoy it. Slowly get up from your chair and begin your day with the mindfulness you have just experienced.

Mindfully Drinking Wine

Another easy opportunity to be mindful is when you are out socialising and having a drink. Most of us like a glass of wine here and there of varying colours, so make sure you are fully present to enjoy it fully. Obviously make sure you drink responsibly, but you will probably find that each glass takes longer to drink as you enjoy it in a way you haven't previously. If you are a wine connoisseur you will naturally be mindful when you are drinking your wine so may as well skip onto the next section now.

Once your first glass of wine has arrived at your table or the bar, and before you've picked it up to taste, pause for a moment and take a breath. Make it an intentional breath but it doesn't need to be obvious. Make sure you notice the breath coming in through your nostrils, filling your chest and then exiting through your mouth. While you're having this breath, consider that this is the first glass along with the start of a nice meal or an evening out with friends, and the rest of the evening is yet to unfold.

Take a quick look at the glass sitting there, what type of glass is it and it's shape. Take note of the wine sitting inside along with the depth of its colour. Just make sure you take in the moment for a while as you will never have the moment again. Now as you pick up the glass notice it's weight and whether it is cold or warm? Watch the wine move in the glass as you hold it and whether the wine clings to the sides of glass at all (has legs). As you bring the glass to your nose, can you notice when your nose picks up the aroma of the wine? Can you recognise any scents or flavours in the wine's bouquet? This is always interesting to discuss with someone else drinking the same wine. Simply by having this conversation about what you can both notice in the bouquet is making you both mindful as you are both experiencing the present.

Now take a sip but don't swallow yet. Move the wine around in your mouth for a while and stay present as your brain picks up the temperature and all the different flavours it can detect. What emotions are you feeling now? Don't be tempted to swallow too quickly, just stay focused on the wine in your mouth and the way it feels for a few seconds. Finally swallow it fully and notice how you feel. Obviously you don't need to do this every time you take a sip of wine but certainly try to make sure you do with the first each time you start to drink. It will help make sure you are in the moment and you will enjoy your wine a great deal more.

Mindful Eating

There is much written about mindful eating and a lot of it just isn't practical when you are trying to live a normal live with a job and a family to juggle. However just incorporating some of the principles into your daily life will help with your mindfulness practice. Many features of mindful eating actually hark back to how people used to eat several generations ago which we seemed to have forgotten or cast aside with the pace of life nowadays. Essentially if you place more focus on mealtimes and the food itself, instead of allowing distractions to grab your attention and that of the people you are eating with, mealtimes become a much more enjoyable experience.

Most people seem to have heard that mindful eating involves eating slowly. There are several reasons for this, but the main reason is to allow your brain to keep up with what is being put into your stomach. It takes around twenty minutes for your body to notify your brain about what you've eaten, which is why a lot of us end up overeating. Often the meal is finished before the brain knows you've even started.

Many of us eat what we routinely do at a meal time, instead of actually listening to the signals we get from our body. This is regardless of whether we are full or still hungry. Generally we do different things on different days requiring more or less energy from our meals but always eating the same amount will lead to overeating or under eating. If you under eat and find yourself hungry a while after your meal you are likely to snack. So just by slowing down your intake, you can ensure that you get what your body needs from a particular meal, no more and no less.

Simple ways to slow down your eating are to make sure you chew each bite twenty five times, ensuring you have completely swallowed one bite before taking another bite and putting down your cutlery between each bite. Talk to whomever you are eating with as it will slow down your eating as you each converse and is much more enjoyable.

Another common problem when it comes to eating is that we listen to what our mind is telling us instead of what our body is telling us about whether it's time to eat or not. Many of us end up eating for many other reasons instead of just when our body tells us we need to eat. Hunger signs to look out for are a grumbling stomach, light-headedness or feeling low on energy. If you are not experiencing these symptoms you should question whether you really need to be eating now. Obviously it's not practical for everyone in the family to eat at only the times their bodies tell them they are hungry, but when it's a mealtime ensure that you are mindful of what your body is telling you about what you are eating. Remember your mind may be telling you to eat but what is your body telling you?

With the way we lead our lives now, preparation for mealtimes has become more difficult. It will take some effort but thinking about meals in advance to make sure you have everything you need before you prepare meals will help ensure you eat healthily and more mindfully. When are searching through an empty kitchen trying to find something to eat or prepare for dinner it will make meals less inspiring and you less inclined to be mindful about them. If you are going to be mindful at mealtimes it becomes a lot easier and more enjoyable when the meal is full of fresh, interesting and flavoursome food.

If and when you do buy your produce in advance, make sure that it is all put away in your fridge, kitchen cabinets and out of sight, and not left lying around attracting your attention. When we see food we get the urge to eat it. Another good tactic is, mindfully controlling where you eat your food, like at the dining table and in the kitchen only. After a while of doing this, not only will meals become more of an enjoyable family experience but eating anywhere else in the house like on the sofa will feel strange and uncomfortable.

Before and as you continue to eat your meal, notice all

the different colours and shapes on your plate. It's so easy to just dive in but just take a moment before each fork full to notice your plate and its contents in a bit of detail. When you place food onto your fork notice the weight as you lift it to your mouth. When you take a bite, notice the texture, temperature and specific flavour of the mouthful.

A great way to be more mindful at mealtimes is to think and discuss everything and everyone that was involved in the delivery of the food to your plate. Think about where it was grown or fed and the people that did this. It was then harvested and distributed, maybe from a far flung place in the world. It then likely was stocked onto a supermarket shelf by somebody else and then put into your shopping trolley by you before being brought home in your car that was fuelled and built by somebody else. Finally it was prepared and cooked by someone in your home so it can be enjoyed by you. Considering all the processes and people involved in all the different aspects of bringing the food to your plate is a great way to exercise your gratitude.

Finally, remove or turn off anything that will distract from focusing on your meal like TVs, tablets and mobile phones. All these can wait until you have finished your meal. Enjoy the experience of the meal itself, the feelings it causes to arise in you along with enjoying your company at the dinner table. Without these kind of distractions you are more likely to be here in the moment, enjoying all the flavours, aromas and company of your friends and family.

Mindful Sitting

You can do this when you first arrive at work or when you sit down to breakfast in the morning. Your intention is to start your day with a few minutes of mindfulness. If you can make this a habit each day and you'll soon be clocking up the mindful minutes in your life. Don't worry if your mind wanders while you're doing this as with all mindfulness practice, so long as you notice your mind has wandered and bring it back to the present moment you are still making positive changes. Not only are you training your mind to focus on what you choose, you are also training your mind to be able to refocus when it wanders.

Make sure you are sitting comfortably in the chair with your back straight and set an intention to do this for a few minutes of your choosing. The more time the better but whatever you can spare is better than none. Place a soft smile on your face and start to bring your attention to your breath wherever you can feel it the most. Do not change your breathing, just allow it to be as it is naturally and just notice and observe it with your mind. Notice the in breaths and the out breaths, and where you feel each one physically. All you are trying to do here is just maintain your focus and attention on your breathing and nothing else. Remember if you mind wanders, and it will, just bring your attention back to your breath, without any criticism or judgement of yourself. Your subconscious is learning each time that you do this, even if you feel consciously that it's not working. It is all adding up.

After a minute or so, turn your attention towards noticing and feeling your legs and buttocks touching the chair or seat. Observe how and where they make contact with the seat and if it is feeling comfortable. If it is uncomfortable focus on exactly where it feels uncomfortable and just hold your attention there without moving if you can. After about another minute, turn your attention to your feet and feel how they make contact to the floor. Notice how you feet feel inside you shoes. Can you notice any pressure from your footwear on the top of your foot, on the heel or toes maybe.

If you choose you can continue with your mindfulness by moving onto noticing sounds you can hear, then maybe any smells you can notice and maybe observe what emotions you are feeling. It's entirely up to you, just remember the point is to be noticing what is happening right now, however you choose to do this.

Mindful Walking

As we've already mentioned, we are all already aware of how important exercise is for our physical health. So why not combine helping improve your physical health and your mental health at the same time. Next time you take a walk anywhere, it could be a walk to the shops or a walk around the local park, make a mental note to be more mindful. If you can, try leaving your mobile phone at home too.

While you walk, consciously notice your breath entering through the nostrils, filling your lungs and then exiting through your mouth. We rarely think about our breath from one day to the next, but without it you wouldn't be here. Take some time to notice how your breath changes as you walk. Do not try to control the breath, just notice it as it happens. Does it increase in frequency and become heavier? This will likely be related to how hard you are pushing yourself as you walk. Try to see whether you can count ten breaths in and ten breaths out without your mind wandering onto another subject.

As you walk, try to notice things that you've not seen on this walk before. There will be hundreds of things that you possibly walk past everyday and don't even notice normally. Notice the shapes and colours of the leaves on different trees as you pass them. Notice the ground under your feet, can you feel the different surfaces through the soles of your shoes? As you change surfaces can you notice the difference in how it feels underfoot, differences in colours and composition? Notice buildings and all the various different types, designs and construction. Take note of window shapes, door colours and roofs.

Particularly if you are walking in a park or the countryside, notice the different sounds that you can hear. Can you hear birds chirping, wind blowing through the tops of trees or maybe the sound of an animal scurrying in the undergrowth. Don't try to identify the bird or animal but just notice the different sounds that you can hear and when they change. You may be able to hear an aeroplane overhead, cars in the distance or children playing.

What can you smell? Can you smell the plants and wildlife around you as you walk? It could be that you notice exhaust fumes from passing vehicles or aromas wafting from shops that you pass. You might notice the aftershave or perfume of a passing stranger. The world around us is full of different smells but often we just don't notice the subtle differences.

Can you feel the temperature on your skin? Is it warm or cold? Can you notice the temperature changes as you walk through the shadows of buildings? Is your temperature changing as you walk? Can you feel a breeze or maybe raindrops on your face. Can you feel the heat from the sun's rays on your back? If it's cold, can you notice your ears and toes getting colder?

How do you feel when you start out on your walk? What emotions can you detect? It could be anything from happiness to sadness but just notice it and don't focus on it. Ask yourself the same question at various points along the walk and when you finish. Does what you see and hear on your journey change how you feel?

Remember that your mind will wander and that is absolutely fine. You are not trying to be mindful for the whole walk, just choose to be mindful at certain points just to practice being mindful. Even if your mind wanders while you are trying to be mindful this is fine too. Just notice it has wandered and come back to trying to be mindful again.

Mindful Running

Many of us run at regular times each week as part of our fitness routine. This is the perfect time to practice being mindful. Once you get going it's very common for your mind to wander off onto a subject that has nothing to do with your run and you end up on autopilot. If you want to improve your time or distance, being mindful will help as it combines your focus on the physical and mental aspects. As you are being more mindful you will notice your breathing and any indications from your body that you are pushing too hard or not hard enough.

Before you head out, take a couple of minutes to take in your surroundings. Notice the temperature and what you can see and hear in the area. Take note of how your body feels, are parts of it feeling tired or fired up and ready for action? How does your clothing feel against your skin? Are your running shoes feeling laced correctly? Notice what emotions and feelings you are experiencing before you start, is it excitement, anxiety or anticipation? Or something else? Do not judge yourself or the conditions, just acknowledge how things are. Becoming familiar with your own body, mind and surroundings should become part of your pre run routine as much as warming up and stretching and could help as part of understanding your performances.

Once you are off and running and without putting yourself in any danger take notice of how your body is feeling. Are your muscles responding as they should as you move? What are are you feeling now? Relieved to be out in the fresh air and out of the office? Is your mind wandering off onto today's or tomorrow's events? As you continue to run try to notice the environment more than normal. It's amazing how much you miss while running. It could be that you notice cars, other runners, all the different surfaces you run over, street names, etc.

Once you settle into the run, notice whether your pace is normal or whether more effort than usual is required. How are your shoulders feeling? Are they loose or tense? Is there any tension anywhere else in the body? If there is, then allow it to release naturally, don't try to do something about it now that you've noticed it and just accept that it is there.

Notice the action of actually running such that as each foot as hits the ground heel first and the other one leaves the ground heel first. Notice your knees lifting in turn as you bring each foot forward. Try not to focus too much on the actual action itself but notice how easy running is with a relaxed mind. Are you starting to feel tiredness in any of your muscles? Is your breathing becoming laboured? Just notice what you are experiencing without making any changes that you wouldn't normally make.

Whether you are running for fun or for fitness, practising mindfulness while running should not be too difficult. After all you are running anyway and why not pay a bit more attention to what you are doing and where you are running, especially if it gives you the opportunity to practice being mindful. You don't need to practice all these techniques to be mindful, but the more you do and the more often you do them, the more mindful you will become overall and your body and mind will reap the rewards.

Mindful Driving

Do not attempt to meditate behind the wheel. Driving can be quite a stressful experience especially in rush-hour, so a way to reduce this stress would surely be welcome. Driving is also an act that doesn't involve much thought of the conscious brain most of the time. How often have you arrived at your destination without being able to remember the journey at all? We are often away somewhere else with our thoughts or tuned into music on the radio.

So when you get in your car take a minute before you start it up to close your eyes and take in the atmosphere of the vehicle and how you are feeling. Set an intention to make this drive a mindful one. When you start the car, put your mobile phone in the glove box and turn off the radio so you are not distracted from being mindful. As you drive and keeping your focus on the road, notice any sounds that you hear from outside the car, like other cars passing in the opposite direction and any sounds that your car is making that you can hear from inside. Notice as many of the buildings and various landscapes that you drive past.

If your mind wanders, mentally note that it has wandered away from mindfully driving and bring your attention back to noticing sounds, seeing the outside world around you and feeling the road through the steering and the pedals. If somebody cuts you up or does something to annoy you, notice what emotions you are feeling and pause before you respond. If your speed creeps above the limit ask yourself why and slow down. When you reach your destination, turn of the car and sit again for minute before exiting the car in a more mindful frame of mind. By doing this you will arrive less stressed and more focused than you normally would.

Mindful Tidiness

Clutter is a distraction for your brain. Although your conscious mind gets used to the clutter and doesn't take in all the details of the world, your subconscious mind takes in everything. By simply tidying up and keeping things tidy and in order, you will notice practising mindfulness is a bit easier. Having clutter and mess around you causes tension in your subconscious. The simpler your world is, the less stressful it is for your subconscious.

A de-cluttered and more open space is a more enjoyable place to be and you can enjoy the purge of all your old junk. A good rule of thumb is, if you haven't used it for three years then get rid of it. As you clear clutter away and dispose of junk you don't use any more, the chances are you will need to have a good clean too. Cleaning is another opportunity to practice your mindfulness of course. When you are cleaning, just clean, don't think about what you are going to do next or listen to music. Focus on exactly what you are doing in this moment. You can focus on the cloth, the vacuum or the broom along with the actions you are using, and the before and after effects of whatever it is you are cleaning.

Clean with compassion and gratitude. You can feel

some gratitude for whatever it is you are cleaning. If it was a gift you can feel gratitude for whoever gave it to you. You can feel compassionate about making your environment a cleaner and more enjoyable place to live. All of this is mindful behaviour and will help with your general well-being.

Half Smiling

In his book The Miracle Of Mindfulness, Thich Nhat Hanh lists and describes many occasions where a half smile can not only help with your mindful practice but help lift your mood very quickly. The science shows that smiling will improve your frame of mind. A relatively well known brain hack is that faking a smile will make you happier so long as you feel it in your eyes!

Wake Up Half Smile

Either have something on your bedside table or hanging on the wall as a reminder so that it will be the first thing you see when you open your eyes. It could be something as simple as a note that just says "smile". Before you move to get out of bed give a half smile for three inhales and exhales. Make sure you maintain your half smile throughout and notice each breath fully.

Free Half Smile

This one can be absolutely anywhere and whenever there is a free moment. You could be standing in a queue, walking to the shops or sitting on the train to work. Take note of something that is not moving or is relatively still and half smile while you focus your attention on your chosen spot. At the same time quietly inhale and exhale three times.

Irritated Half Smile

If you notice you've become irritated, give yourself a half smile and hold it for three inhales and exhales while taking notice of your breathing.

Music Half Smile

When you are listening to some music, pay full attention to the rhythm, words, music and sentiments being conveyed while holding a half smile.

Breathing

Bellow Breathing

Originally a yogic breathing technique this is a stimulating way of breathing and is helpful for raising energy and increasing alertness. This is a good technique for next time you feel like reaching for a coffee. It has also been suggested that this breathing technique can boost your metabolism and help digestive strength. This breathing technique is performed in rounds of 10, 20 and 30 breaths with a 15-30 second break between each round.

1. Make sure you are sitting up straight with you mouth closed but relaxed. Take a few deep breaths through your nose and exhale through your nose.

2. Breath in and out through your nose as quickly as you can ten times in the first round.

3. Make sure you are sitting upright and straight. The breath needs to come from your diaphragm. Evident by your stomach moving in and out with your breathing.

4. Allow your breathing to return to normal for 15-30 seconds before starting the next round.

Bellows breathing should be completely safe but if you find that you are getting light headed either wait longer between rounds or build up the rounds more gradually over several sessions. Bellows breathing is perfect to give you a kick start in the morning or after lunch when you are starting to flag at work.

4-7-8 Breathing

If you're having trouble getting off to sleep or are feeling anxious about something this a breathing technique that will likely help in both situations. It has the effect of dulling the nervous system and the more you do it the stronger the effects will be. Place the tip of your tongue onto the back of your front top teeth and exhale through your mouth.

1. Breath in silently through your nose for four seconds.

2. Hold your breath for another seven seconds.

3. Finally exhale through your mouth (keeping the tip of your tongue on your teeth) making a woosh sound as the breath exits for eight seconds.

Repeat steps 1-3 four times. This can be extended to eight times once you become more comfortable. If you feel light headed please stop and let it pass. If you struggle with amount of time of each or one step, you can half the times but it is important to maintain the 4-7-8 ratio.

Counting Breath

Breath counting is simply the act of counting your breaths in and out. Sit up straight, close your eyes and take a few deep breaths before you start. Simply count your exhales to yourself. With the first inhale and exhale say to yourself "one", with the second say to yourself "two" and so on. When you get to "five" then start again at "one".

Only count your exhales and if you go past "five" without realising your mind has wandered. If at any point while you are counting you realise your mind has wandered then acknowledge it has happened and then start again at "one" on the next exhale. Continue to do this for around ten minutes.

You Have Been Meditating

As can be seen above there are no end of ways you can be mindful throughout your day and the more you can do, the more mindful you will become. It is important to remember that everyone questions whether they are really noticing the benefits of mindfulness from time to time. It is only after you have been doing for a while that will really notice the differences yourself, although others will likely notice the change in your demeanour and attitude before you do.

Meditate

Verb | Med - i – tate

1. Engaging in contemplation or concentration
2. Giving your attention to one thing

As can be seen from the dictionary definition above, if you have been performing any of the techniques earlier in this chapter you have been engaging in a form of meditation already. Meditation is purely the act of concentrating on one particular thing, often in mindfulness this is your breathing or sensations that you are feeling right now. There are lots of other forms of meditation but the beauty of mindfulness meditation is you can do it at any time while you're going about your day to day business.

If ever you are considering quitting your mindful practice try to take it as an opportunity to be mindful and understand why you feel this way right now. Remember it's not a competition and everyone takes to it differently, although everyone will benefit from being more mindful.

If you take this opportunity to embrace formal meditation then you will notice the differences in yourself a lot sooner. Formal meditation isn't much different to what we've seen so far in this chapter except it is just the act of formally putting aside time to do mindfulness practice and only mindfulness practice. It's worth noting that formal meditation has been proven to increase grey matter in the brain and is favoured as technique for calming and training focus by almost all of the most successful people on the planet. Formal meditation is also shown to reduce your overreactions and help reduce your ego. By practising formal mindfulness meditations regularly you will notice a quicker change in your state of mind than if you just perform daily actions in a mindful way.

10

FORMAL MEDITATION

RATHER THAN BEING YOUR THOUGHTS
AND EMOTIONS, BE THE AWARENESS
BEHIND THEM.
ECKHART TOLLE

Many of us have preconceptions about what formal meditation is and which sort of people formally meditate. The fact that you are reading this suggests that you are open minded already and interested in improving your quality of life. Put aside what you think you already know about formal meditation and which sort of people formally meditate for a while. You will likely be surprised how easy it is to do, the benefits it provides and how your life can be changed for good by knowing a bit more about formal meditation.

Mindfulness meditation is just consciously spending time to improve your mindfulness. This doesn't mean it has to be a formal meditation as it can be done at any time from queueing in shops, eating or simply while you're walking down the street as discussed in the last chapter. Formal meditation is the act of putting aside some time to specifically meditate on mindfulness. This chapter is all about formal meditation as it allows you to concentrate more on your mindfulness practice. For the rest of this chapter we'll just refer to it as meditation. Saves ink and the number of words you need to read.

Meditation isn't about becoming some new age hippy or starting to believe in some new religion, it is purely a way for you to get to know your own mind in a way you don't currently. You don't need to chant mantras or wear some weird tie dye clothing, all it takes is some patience and a small amount of perseverance for you to start discovering your own mind. It takes a level of curiosity to give it a go and a few minutes sitting down concentrating - that's about it. Mindfulness meditation is just a tool to get to know your mind so you can better understand what thoughts, memories, emotions, doubts, etc. are influencing and clouding your view of the world, and what potentially is holding you back from enjoying more of your life.

Most people do not have meditation as part of their lives and it can seem quite intimidating if you don't fully understand what it is, or have some preformed opinions of what it involves. It is unfamiliar to you so it's natural to be wary, but if you didn't try anything new you would never move forward with anything in your life. You are going to give this a try because your intention is to try to improve yourself and your quality of life.

Something to bear in mind is that many of the world's most successful people have meditation as part of their life in one form or another. You have nothing to lose by trying mindfulness meditation and everything to gain. You do it in private so no-one else needs to know you are meditating if that's what you'd prefer. Meditation can be performed by anyone with all the guided meditations that exist online or as part of apps, so there is no excuse for not giving it a try.

Probably the most common complaint is that there isn't enough time in my life for meditation. By saying you don't have enough time, you are effectively saying that you don't have a few minutes each day to help reduce your stress levels and improve your general well-being. When you have reduced stress levels and improved well-being you will notice more of life so in some ways gain more time to live life. Also as mindful meditation will help improve your focus, make you more attentive and more relaxed so you will be able to complete tasks with greater efficiency gaining even more time that would not previously have had.

You may believe that mindfulness meditation will be boring, well if we are honest about it, anything can be boring if you allow it to be. Boredom is usually born out of restlessness that there could be something more interesting that you could be doing in a given moment. Mediation can be boring at times but you will continue to do it as you know that the benefits it brings will ensure that the more interesting moments will likely become even more interesting as a result. Remember you are trying to improve yourself and understand yourself. That takes some form of commitment from you as no one else is going to do it for you.

You may believe that mindfulness meditation is too religious or spiritual. Mindfulness meditation is only about understanding yourself, it's not about becoming religious in some way or having to believe in spirits, gods or higher beings. Ideally you should end up just believing in yourself more than you did before you started mindfulness meditation. In fact, mindfulness meditation is the reverse of spiritual and religious meditations as it does not allow you to escape to another world or dimension, the whole point is you learn to be here in the present wherever and whatever that is in reality.

Mindfulness meditation in whatever form it takes is about training your attention to focus on one thing for a chosen amount of time without getting distracted. Even if your mind wanders this is not considered failure, it is just completely normal for all of us. Another cornerstone of mindfulness is acceptance, so when your mind wanders, you just accept that it has happened and then return focus back to the intended subject of attention without any criticism of yourself.

Most of us don't know how to meditate and just the thought of it can make you feel uncomfortable. This is just the fear of the unknown and if you continue reading it will no longer be an unknown to you. There is nothing to worry about as all you will be doing is exploring your own mind and trying to improve the way it functions. You will also notice that when you start to practice your mindful meditations that other people will notice the difference in you and will likely comment. When you reveal that you have started meditating you will be surprised how many other people also meditate but without telling others until someone else admits to it.

The key thing to remember is that mindfulness meditation is about being curious about how your mind works, calming yourself emotionally and trying to understand yourself better so you can improve. You should become an explorer and adventurer that is trying to map and explore your mind. Some parts might be dark while others will make you light up with joy, it's just part of the journey and it's one that you will ultimately enjoy and help lead to improvements in your general well-being amongst the many other benefits.

There are many different forms of mindfulness meditation and you may find that one works better for you than others. You might find that you cannot get on with a particular form of mindfulness meditation. If this is the case, just accept that this type of meditation doesn't work for you and explore other mindfulness meditations. Everyone is different and it is just what works for you and whatever technique produces the best results for you.

You will also find that when you start to look into mindfulness meditations further that some help with different types of feelings and different circumstances. Experiment with all that you come across, you may find that one works better than others for you. We will cover a few forms of mindfulness meditations here to get you started but you should do your own research to find what works best for you.

Guided Meditations

Guided meditations are the best place to start if you have never tried meditation before. Guided meditations are very popular and many people only ever use guided mindfulness meditations. If it works for you, stick with it.

A guided meditation is just a meditation where you are

verbally led through what to do, when you need to do it, by an instructor or teacher. All you need to do is follow the instructions that you are given by the teacher or instructor. The process often involves, monitoring your breathing with your mind, some form of visualisation and often listening to your senses.

There are many apps that will help with guided meditations, many of them for free. Another good source of guided meditations is YouTube™, these are all free and cover just about every subject imaginable. So take some time to find the right meditations for you. You will likely find that there are some meditations that you come back to over and over again once you've found them.

Scheduling Meditation

Study after study shows that if you put aside a regular amount of time each day for a consistent period of time (usually eight weeks in the studies) that there is a noticeable difference in the calmness, feelings of well-being and positivity. The amount of time you put aside each day can vary from five minutes to many more but the key is repeating the action day after day, i.e. making part of your normal daily routine. Most people seem to find that first thing in the morning is best as it sets them up for the day. However others prefer to meditate before bed to calm their mind before going to sleep. Whenever you choose to do it it should be regular.

You can choose to do different types of mindfulness meditations for each session to save getting bored of repeating the same meditation everyday. You'll see some basic meditations explained later but install an app or search the internet as there are so many to choose from.

Obviously life doesn't always allow you to do it everyday and this is completely fine and it is not a reason to criticise yourself or see a missed day as a failure, just continue the next day as if you haven't missed any. Every session is a benefit and you cannot change the past, so just let it go if you missed a session. Think of your daily meditation as your own refresh button, so if you miss a refresh, just refresh yourself the next day or later in the same day.

Some suggestions for times to schedule your daily mediation.

- **First thing in the morning** Get up, go to the toilet and do whatever you need to do in the bathroom and then come back to your bedroom and meditate.

- **During your lunch break** When you break for lunch at work take a walk to the local park each day. You can pick up your lunch on the way there or way back. Sit on a bench and perform your meditation there. You could just pop out to the car park and just sit in your car for a few minutes while you meditate. Or alternatively you can just sit in your office chair before heading off to the canteen.

- **After work** Before you head home in the rush hour, take a couple of minutes sitting in your car before you start it up and meditate. The journey will almost definitely be less stressful. While standing at the station waiting for your train each night you can meditate then.

- **Before bed** Get ready for bed and make meditation the last thing you do before getting into bed. Be careful if you are tempted to do it in bed that you don't fall asleep as you won't receive the benefits.

These are just a few ideas to show you how easy it is to incorporate mindfulness meditation into your day.

There are so many gaps in our day when we are mindless, so why not turn that moment each day to your advantage. The biggest tip is to make sure that you do it after the same action that you perform everyday to make it as habitual as the action that it follows.

Formal Meditations

There are many mindfulness meditations that you can do covering a wide variety of subjects and in varying lengths of time too. We all come to mindfulness from different perspectives and we all have our own issues that mindfulness can help us understand further and hopefully improve.

For the rest of this chapter we will run through a few of the most common and easiest mindfulness meditations so you can see how easy they are. Don't be deceived by how simple they look on the page as they really do work if you commit to practising meditation regularly. As mentioned earlier on, when you start you will likely find it easier to use guided meditations from the internet instead of having to memorise what is written here.

Breathing Space Meditation

Breathing space meditation is one of the simplest and easiest meditations to do as it is simply just a case of focusing on your breathing. It can be done in most positions but preferably it should be done while sitting down. Ideally you will do this for a minimum of five minutes but do more if you can.

You will probably find it easier to do while your eyes are closed but it can be done with your eyes open too. This technique can be used at any time when you start to notice feelings of stress or anxiety as it will have a calming effect.

You can set an alarm when doing this for the desired length or just do it for long enough for you to know that it has had an effect on how you're feeling if you are doing it in a stressful moment.

1. **Get comfortable** Make sure you are in a comfortable position. Ideally this is sitting with you back straight, but you can do this standing too.

2. **Notice** Breathe normally while you take a moment to notice the shape of your body sitting in your chair or on the floor. Notice the connection and where the weight is connecting with the chair or floor. If you are standing notice where the weight is in your feet and

where the pressure is on the soles of your feet.

3. **Breathing** Now notice your breathing, in and out as it happens naturally. Do not try to change your breathing at all. Notice where you can feel the breath in your body. It could be the feel of the air coming in through your nostrils or on the back of your throat. You may notice your chest and / or abdomen rising and falling with each breath. Notice the timings of each breath, inhale, pause and the exhale, and the gap between the end of one breath and start of the next.

4. **Wandering mind** Your mind will wander, everyone's does. When it does, just take note that it has and bring your attention back to breathing again. You might notice that your mind has wandered for a long time. It doesn't matter, just bring your attention back to breathing again, it's all part of the process. As time progresses you will notice that your mind wanders less and you notice when it has after shorter periods. When you do notice your mind has wandered off onto something other than breathing just say to yourself "wandered" or "thinking" or some other term, and then

bring your focus back to the breath.

5. **Notice again** Finally when your time is up, take a few moments to notice the shape of your body and your connections with the chair or ground again.

Expanding Awareness Meditation

Training your awareness is an important part of being more mindful. The more aware you are of anything in the current moment the more mindful you are. This particular meditation is focused on your thoughts. You can apply the same techniques to focusing on your feelings and emotions, to sounds or to how your body is feeling.

This meditation can be done for around five minutes or more if you can. As with all mindfulness meditation, the more you do the more you benefit. With this meditation you should notice what stories your mind is telling you in contrast to what the reality actually is. The more that you perform this meditation or similar meditations you should start to notice thought patterns, whether they are good or bad. When you have learned how to detect these thought patterns it is then up to you to decide how to respond instead of blindly following them down a rabbit hole.

1. **Get comfortable** Ideally you should do this while sitting comfortably in a chair with your back straight.

2. **Notice** Take a few deep breaths while you spend a bit of time noticing the shape of your body and how and where it connects with the chair. Notice what emotions and feelings you are currently experiencing. Also notice how busy your mind is. Is it racing or is it calm? Allow your breathing to return to your body's natural rhythm.

3. **Awareness of Breath** Spend the next minute or so just focusing your attention on your breathing. Apply a curiosity to the breathing as if it's the first time you've noticed it. Notice where you can feel the breath in your body. It could be the feel of the air coming in through your nostrils or on the back of your throat. You may notice your chest and / or abdomen rising and falling with each breath. Notice the timings of each breath, inhale, pause and the exhale, and the gap between the end of one breath and start of the next.

4. **Awareness of body** Now spend at least the

next minute noticing your body. Does it ache and can you feel tightness or pressure anywhere? Do you have any itches? If the mind wanders while you're doing this, just acknowledge that it has and bring attention back to your body.

5. **Awareness of Sounds** Take the next minute to pay attention to what sounds you can hear. Do not try to label what is producing the sound but instead just notice the sound itself. See if you can notice sounds that you would not normally hear here. Once again if the mind wanders, just acknowledge it and return back to focusing on the sounds that you can hear.

6. **Awareness of Thoughts** Now just watch the thoughts as they come in your mind. If the subject changes, make a mental note of the new subject. Even thinking "Is this a thought?", is a thought. Remind yourself that these are just thoughts as they come and go through your mind.

7. **Notice again** Finally when your time is up take a few moments to notice your breathing again with the inhalations and exhalations and

how it affects the shape of your body.

Body Scan Meditation

The body scan meditation is about understanding exactly what is going on with your body. It is not about improving how things are or about trying to make things different to how they are. This is "you time" so just allow yourself to relax and just let things be what they are.

The body scan meditation will take around half an hour, so make sure you will not be disturbed by anyone or your phone. Also make sure that you are wearing loose clothing or the clothing you are wearing is not too tight anywhere.

1. **Get comfortable** This meditation is done lying down so make sure you are in a comfortable position before starting, but not so comfortable that you will fall asleep. Ensure your legs are out straight and apart. If it's too uncomfortable to maintain this position for half an hour without moving you can place a pillow under your knees. Your arms should be down beside you with palms facing upwards.

2. **Notice** Spend a few moments taking note of

where your body makes contact with the bed and feel the weight of your body pressing down on it. Move up and down your body a few times noticing each point.

3. **Breathing** Now notice your breathing, in and out as it happens naturally. Do not try to change your breathing at all. Notice where you can feel the breath in your body. It could be the feel of the air coming in through your nostrils or on the back of your throat. You may notice your chest and / or abdomen rising and falling with each breath. Notice the timings of each breath, inhale, pause and the exhale, and the gap between the end of one breath and start of the next.

4. **Left foot toes** Move your attention to the big toe on your left foot. Does it feel cold or warm? Can you feel your sock or air movement around it? Now move your attention to each toe in turn on your left foot asking the same questions. If with any toe you cannot notice anything, make a note in your head that you couldn't feel anything.

5. **Breathe** Now breathe in through the toes on

your left foot. As you inhale imagine that there are holes at the end of your toes that allows the air into your body through those toes, imagine the air travelling up your leg towards your lungs and then exhale normally through your mouth. After a minute or so of breathing like this return to normal breathing.

6. **Left foot** Now direct your attention to the sole, ball and heel of your left foot, can you notice any sensations? Is the bottom of your foot feeling tired at all? Move your attention to the sides, top of your foot and ankle. Do you notice anything?

7. **Breathe** Now breathe in through the bottom of your left foot. As you inhale imagine the air coming into your body through holes in the bottom of your foot, imagine the air travelling up past your ankle, through your leg towards your lungs and then exhale normally through your mouth. After a minute or so of breathing like this return to normal breathing.

8. **Left lower leg** Turn the focus of your attention to the left shin and whether you can feel anything. Can feel your trousers against

your skin or the air moving around your leg? Move attention to the calf, can you feel exactly where it is touching the bed? Is it feeling tired or aching?

9. **Breathe** Now breathe in through the shin and calf of your left leg. As you inhale imagine the air coming into your body through holes in the front and back of your lower left leg, imagine the air travelling up past your knee towards your lungs and then exhale normally through your mouth. After a minute or so of breathing like this return to normal breathing.

10. **Left knee and thigh** Direct your attention to your left knee now. Do you notice any pains, aches or any other sensations. If you have a pillow under your knees, can you feel where the back of the knee touches the pillow. Focus on your thigh, does it feel tight or relaxed? Can you notice where it makes contact with clothing, covers or the sheets of the bed?

11. **Breathe** Now breathe in through the left knee. As you inhale imagine the air coming into your body through holes just below your kneecap and then moving up your upper leg towards

your lungs and then exhale normally through your mouth. After a minute or so of breathing like this return to normal breathing.

12. **Right foot toes** Now take your attention to the other leg and to the big toe on your right foot. Does it feel cold or warm? Can you feel your sock or air movement around it? Now move your attention to each toe in turn on your right foot asking the same questions. If with any toe you cannot notice anything, make a note in your head that you couldn't feel anything.

13. **Breathe** Now breathe in through your the toes on your right foot. As you inhale imagine that there are holes at the end of your toes that allows the air into your body through those toes, imagine the air travelling up your leg towards your lungs and then exhale normally through your mouth. After a minute or so of breathing like this return to normal breathing.

14. **Right foot** Now direct your attention to the sole, ball and heel of your right foot, can you notice any sensations? Is the bottom of your foot feeling tired at all? Move your attention to

the sides, top of your foot and ankle. Do you notice anything?

15. **Breathe** Now breathe in through the bottom of your right foot. As you inhale imagine the air coming into your body through holes in the bottom of your foot, imagine the air travelling up past your ankle, through your leg towards your lungs and then exhale normally through your mouth. After a minute or so of breathing like this return to normal breathing.

16. **Right lower leg** Turn the focus of your attention to the right shin and whether you can feel anything. Can you feel your trousers against your skin or the air moving around your leg? Move attention to the calf, can you feel where exactly it is touching the bed? Is it feeling tired or aching?

17. **Breathe** Now breathe in through the shin and calf of your right leg. As you inhale imagine the air coming into your body through holes in the front and back of your lower right leg, imagine the air travelling up past your knee towards your lungs and then exhale normally through your mouth. After a minute or so of breathing

like this return to normal breathing.

18. **Right knee and thigh** Direct your attention to your right knee now. Do you notice any pains, aches or any other sensations. If you have a pillow under your knees, can you feel where the back of the knee touches the pillow. Focus on your right thigh, does it feel tight or relaxed? Can you notice where it makes contact with clothing, covers or the sheets of the bed?

19. **Breathe** Now breathe in through the right knee. As you inhale imagine the air coming into your body through holes just below your kneecap and then moving up your upper leg towards your lungs and then exhale normally through your mouth. After a minute or so of breathing like this return to normal breathing.

20. **Both legs** Now think about your left leg as a whole and notice whether it feels any different to your right leg and vice versa.

21. **Breathe** Now breathe in through the hips, pelvis, buttocks and lower organs. As you inhale imagine the air coming into your body

through holes all over this area filling them with oxygen and then moving up towards your lungs and then exhale normally through your mouth. After a minute or so of breathing like this return to normal breathing.

22. **Lower torso, lower abdomen and lower back** Do you notice any aches or pains in your lower back? Can you feel your lower abdomen rising and falling with each breath that you take? Do you notice any signs of emotions emanating from this area of your body?

23. **Breathe** Now breathe in through the lower back. As you inhale imagine the air coming into your body through holes at your lower back, filling this area of your body with life giving oxygen and then moving up towards your lungs and then exhale normally through your mouth. After a minute or so of breathing like this return to normal breathing.

24. **Chest and upper back** Move attention now to your rib cage. Can you feel it rising and falling with your breathing? Offer some gratitude that your lungs, heart and other organs are giving you life and keeping you

alive. Do you feel any emotions coming from your heart area?

25. **Breathe** Now breathe in through the heart. As you inhale imagine the air coming into your body through a hole in your chest in front of your heart filling the heart with life, and then exhale normally through your mouth. After a minute or so of breathing like this return to normal breathing.

26. **Fingers and hands** Move your attention to the fingers and hands on both arms noticing any sensations. Can you feel any air movement around your fingers? Are both hands the same temperature?

27. **Breathe** Now breathe in through the fingertips. As you inhale imagine the air coming in through the tips of all your fingers, up your arms and into your chest and then exhale normally through your mouth. After a minute or so of breathing like this return to normal breathing.

28. **Arms** Take your attention now to both lower arms. Do you feel air movement around them.

Can you notice where they are in contact with clothing, covers and the bed? Move onto noticing any sensations in your upper arms.

29. **Breathe** Now breathe in through the forearms. As you inhale imagine the air coming in through the fronts of your forearms, up your arms, past your elbows and into your chest and then exhale normally through your mouth. After a minute or so of breathing like this return to normal breathing.

30. **Shoulders** Now taking the focus of your attention to your shoulders. Do you feel any tension at all? Are they tight or relaxed?

31. **Breathe** Now breathe in through the upper back. As you inhale imagine the air coming into your body between your shoulder blades, moving through your shoulders and into your chest and then exhale normally through your mouth. After a minute or so of breathing like this return to normal breathing.

32. **Neck and lower jaw** Bring your attention to your neck now. Can you feel how it is supporting your head? And where it touches

the bed or pillow? Can you notice the temperature of the bed or pillow against your skin? Moving onto your lower jaw, is it clenched or relaxed?

33. **Head** Focus your attention on your lips and notice any sensations they are picking up. Move onto your nose and notice the air entering and passing through your nose as you breathe. Focus on your eyes behind your closed eyelids and what sensations are occurring. Now does your forehead feel tight or loose and relaxed. Finally concentrate on the top of your head and whether you can feel anything here.

34. **Breathe** For the next few minutes imagine holes in the soles of your feet and a hole in the top of your head. As you inhale imagine the air coming in through the bottom of your feet and passing up your body into your chest.

As you exhale imagine that the air is being pushed up from your chest, through your neck and out through the top of your head. Continue to do this for another couple of minutes, then reverse the process. Imagine air is being sucked in through the top of your head as you inhale. Then push the air through your body and out through the soles of your feet as you exhale.

35. **Notice** Take a minute or so to just observe your natural breathing and notice how your body feels, any feelings you are experiencing and any thoughts that are passing through your mind.

36. **Acknowledge** Finally acknowledge and appreciate that you have given this time to yourself to be with yourself.

Loving Kindness Meditation

The loving kindness meditation is relaxing and ideal for calming the mind. The loving kindness meditation is about feeling unconditional love and what it feels like to share love unconditionally. Expect nothing in return, just the warm feelings of giving love to yourself and others.

The loving kindness meditation doesn't take very long. Five to ten minutes is enough so it is ideal before you go to bed. Sit in a comfortable position and close your eyes.

1. **Deep breathe** Take five deep breaths and notice your body relaxing further as you exhale each time.

2. **Breathe naturally** Now allow your breath to return to its normal rhythm while you take a moment to notice the shape of your body sitting in your chair or on the floor. Notice the connection and where the weight is connecting with the chair or floor. If you are standing, notice where the weight is in your feet and where the pressure is on the soles of your feet.

3. **Focus on your heart** Now move your attention to your heart and chest. Do you notice any sensations? Place both hands over your heart area.

4. **Remember a good time** Now think about a time when you felt loved, warm, happy and content. Notice the feelings of warmth, happiness, love and contentment. Allow yourself a half smile while you continue to think about this moment for a couple of minutes.

5. **Share with another** Think of someone you

are close to. Imagine the feelings of warmth, love and happiness starting to radiate from your heart space and out of your body. Imagine that they are being received by this other person and how good it feels to share these feelings without expecting anything back in return for a few minutes.

6. **Share with all** Now imagine that your feelings of warmth, love and happiness are radiating and spreading further and further with each breath you take. They are spreading further and further around the globe. Notice how good it feels to share these feelings freely with anyone that they come into contact with, whoever they are.

7. **Notice** Finally take a minute or so to just observe your natural breathing and notice how your body feels, any feelings you are experiencing and any thoughts that are passing through your mind now.

11

WHAT ARE YOU WAITING FOR?

PEOPLE HAVE A HARD TIME
LETTING GO OF THEIR SUFFERING.
OUT OF FEAR OF THE UNKNOWN,
THEY PREFER SUFFERING
THAT IS FAMILIAR.

THICH NHAT HANH

You now know what mindfulness can do for you and your life, you understand that it isn't some kind of woo woo activity and you know how to do it. Either by being more mindful while going about your life moment to moment or by formally meditating to increase the speed of your mindfulness, learning and knowledge of yourself.

It's over to you now. You know all that mindfulness can do and what's involved in being more mindful. It's just a case of putting in a bit of effort and seeing for yourself what the rewards are. Don't forget to set yourself small achievable targets initially, like being mindful for a week, and then before you know it, you'll have been doing it for several weeks and forming the habits that will set you up for life.

Get out of your mind now and get on with giving it a go so you start noticing the improvements to your life. No doubt some of you have got this far and are thinking that your life doesn't need any mindfulness. If this is true, then well done, you have done better than most of us. However, just by adding some mindfulness into your life you can probably make it even better than it is already, it doesn't cost you a penny, and no-one else needs to know you've even tried.

I expect some of you are thinking that I am going to give this a go, starting tomorrow morning. This isn't very mindful thinking, get into the moment now, as there will never be the perfect time to start anything, let alone practising being mindful. Conditions will never be exactly right or perfect, so don't put it off and skip back to some examples and start right now. If you plan to start formally meditating then do your research now. Go on the internet and find a five minute mindfulness breathing meditation. Bookmark it ready for when you start your first meditation. This way you won't spend ages trying to find one instead of actually meditating.

I hope you found this book helpful in some way, even if you don't end up actively being more mindful.

What happened in the past is in your memory. What is going to happen in the future is in your imagination. It is only the present moment that isn't inside your mind, so enjoy as much of the present as you can, it's the only time you really have.

NOTES

As mentioned in the introduction I have read many books, articles and blogs about mindfulness while trying to understand mindfulness for me and hopefully you now. Below you will find the books, articles and blogs that I have read or come across. Hopefully they will prove useful to you.

1. Mindfulness for Dummies - Shamash Alidina
2. The Miracle Of Mindfulness - Thich Nhat Hanh
3. Mindfulness: The Most Effective Techniques - Ian Tuhovsky
4. Mindfulness Without Meditation - Shea Matthew Fisher
5. Mindfulness At Work In A Week - Clara Seeger
6. The Little Book of Mindfulness - Patrizia Collard
7. Mindfulness: Mindfulness for Beginners - Michael Williams
8. The Power of Empathy - Arthur P. Ciaramicoli
9. Emotional Intelligence: 3 Manuscripts - Ryan James
10. Emotional Intelligence: Mastery - Eric Jordan
11. How To Control Your Emotions: Quick Results Guide – HteBooks
12. Self Compassion & Radical Forgiveness - Simon Rothlein
13. Self Compassion - Kristin Neff
14. How to Forgive - Faith Arley
15. An Introduction to Mindfulness - Mindfulness: 100+ Amazing Mindfulness Tips, Exercises & Resources. Bonus: 200+ Mindfulness Quotes to Live By! (Mindfulness for Beginners, Mindfulness Meditation, Yoga & Mindfulness, Anxiety & Mindfulness) by Kevin Gise
16. What is Mindfulness - Mindful.org https://www.mindful.org/what-is-mindfulness/
17. How Gratitude Changes You and Your Brain - Mindful.org https://www.mindful.org/gratitude-changes-brain/
18. Using Mindfulness Meditation to Overcome Anxiety - BeBrainfit.com https://bebrainfit.com/mindfulness-meditation-anxiety/
19. 9 Ways Mindfulness Reduces Stress - Mindful.org https://www.mindful.org/9-ways-mindfulness-reduces-stress/

20. How Mindfulness Beats Job Stress and Burnout - Mindful.org
https://www.mindful.org/mindfulness-beats-job-stress-burnout/

21. Little Book of Mindfulness by Rebecca Howden and Medibank -
https://www.medibank.com.au/livebetter/app/uploads/Little-Book-Of-Mindfulness.pdf

22. The 23 Amazing Health Benefits of Mindfulness for Body and Brain -
PositivePsychologyProgram.com
https://positivepsychologyprogram.com/benefits-of-mindfulness/

23. Randomized-controlled trial of mindfulness-based cancer recovery
versus supportive expressive group therapy among distressed breast
cancer survivors (MINDSET): long- term follow-up results
http://onlinelibrary.wiley.com/doi/10.1002/pon.4150/epdf

24. The Science of Meditation's Effects on Aging - HuffingtonPost.com
https://www.huffingtonpost.com/sonimacom/the-science-of-meditations-effects-on-aging_b_8688678.html

25. The Neuroscience of Mindfulness Meditation and Pain Relief -
PsychologyToday.com https://www.psychologytoday.com/blog/the-athletes-way/201511/the-neuroscience-mindfulness-meditation-and-pain-relief

26. Mindfulness For Pain Relief In 5 Simple Steps - MrsMindfulness.com
https://mrsmindfulness.com/mindfulness-meditation-for-pain-relief-in-simple-5-steps/

27. How to Introduce Mindfulness to our Friends - LondonMindful.com
https://www.londonmindful.com/blog/how-to-introduce-mindfulness-to-our-friends/

28. In the Moment With Emotions: Mindfulness and Emotional
Intelligence - PositivePsychologyProgram.com
https://positivepsychologyprogram.com/mindfulness-emotional-intelligence/

29. 3 Stages to Learning Mindfulness and Gaining Control of Your
Emotions -GoalCast.com https://www.goalcast.com/2017/08/03/3-stages-building-mindfulness-gaining-control-emotions/

30. Mindfulness Is Control - PsychologyToday.com
https://www.psychologytoday.com/blog/in-control/201604/mindfulness-is-control

31. Mindfulness, It can be easy to rush through life without stopping to
notice much - NHS.uk https://www.nhs.uk/Conditions/stress-anxiety-depression/Pages/mindfulness.aspx

32. Laughing Your Way to Mindfulness - HuffingtonPost.com
https://www.huffingtonpost.com/debbie-woodbury/laughter-

mindfulness_b_3038539.html

33. Don't Look Insecure: 6 Ways to Change Behavior and Be Confident - Emily Roberts MA, LPC - HealthyPlace.com https://www.healthyplace.com/blogs/buildingselfesteem/2017/06/dont-look-insecure-6-ways-to-change-behavior-and-be-confident/

34. Mindfulness Can Increase Self-Confidence - Emily Roberts MA, LPC - HealthyPlace.com https://www.healthyplace.com/blogs/buildingselfesteem/2013/03/how-mindfulness-can-increase-self-confidence/

35. Why Mindfulness Helps You Sleep And Sleep Makes You Mindful - Georgia James - HuffingtonPost.co.uk - http://www.huffingtonpost.co.uk/entry/why-sleep-mindfulness-and-wellness-go-hand-in-hand_uk_57e8f98be4b004d4d86343bd

36. 5 Ways to Build Resilience Every Day - Shamash Alidina - Mindful.org https://www.mindful.org/5-ways-build-resilience-every-day/

37. Happiness Is an Inside Job - Margaret Paul, Ph.D. - HuffingtonPost.com https://www.huffingtonpost.com/margaret-paul-phd/happiness-is-an-inside-jo_1_b_6734960.html

38. 10 Ways Mindfulness Has Made Me Happier - Sheila Bayliss - everyday-Mindfulness.org https://www.everyday-mindfulness.org/10-ways-mindfulness-has-made-me-happier/

39. Mindfulness: Has Your Ego Slipped Inside Your Witness? - Nancy Colier - HuffingtonPost.com https://www.huffingtonpost.com/nancy-colier/mindfulness-has-your-ego-_b_4670177.html

40. It's Not Mindfulness Without Kindness - Shamash Alidina - Mindful.org https://www.mindful.org/its-not-mindfulness-without-kindness/

41. How Gratitude Leads to a Happier Life - Melanie Greenberg Ph.D. - PsychologyToday.com https://www.psychologytoday.com/blog/the-mindful-self-express/201511/how-gratitude-leads-happier-life

42. Five Ways Mindfulness Makes Your Relationship Happier - Melanie Greenberg Ph.D. - PsychologyToday.com https://www.psychologytoday.com/blog/the-mindful-self-express/201706/five-ways-mindfulness-makes-your-relationship-happier

43. Deep Listening - David Rome - Mindful.org https://www.mindful.org/deep-listening/

44. How Mindfulness Can Save Your Relationship - Lisa Firestone - HuffingtonPost.com https://www.huffingtonpost.com/lisa-

firestone/mindfulness-relationships_b_3333709.html

45. Empathy 101 - Daniel Goleman - LinkedIn.com
https://www.linkedin.com/pulse/20130929085735-117825785-empathy-101/

46. Three reasons why mindfulness meditation helps relationships - Marsha Lucas Ph.D. - PsychologyToday.com
https://www.psychologytoday.com/blog/rewire-your-brain-love/201001/three-reasons-why-mindfulness-meditation-helps-relationships

47. Do Mindful People Have a Stronger Sense of Self? - Kira M. Newman - Mindful.org - https://www.mindful.org/mindful-people-stronger-sense-self/

48. 7 Ways Mindfulness Improves Your Performance At Work - Morgan Dix - AboutMeditation.com
http://aboutmeditation.com/mindfulness-at-work/

49. Three Benefits to Mindfulness at Work - Jeremy Adam Smith - Mindful.org https://www.mindful.org/three-benefits-to-mindfulness-at-work/

50. 6 Benefits of Incorporating Mindfulness at Work - Cara Newlon - MentalFloss.com http://mentalfloss.com/article/76310/6-benefits-incorporating-mindfulness-work

51. Mindfulness in the Workplace: Benefits, Risks, Complexities - David Brendel - HuffingtonPost.com
https://www.huffingtonpost.com/david-brendel/integrating-executive-coa_b_9065164.html

52. Nine Essential Qualities of Mindfulness - Melanie Greenberg Ph.D. - PsychologyToday.com https://www.psychologytoday.com/blog/the-mindful-self-express/201202/nine-essential-qualities-mindfulness

53. Mindfulness Can Improve Your Running Experience: 4 Tips to Get Started - Marisa Zeppieri - RunSmartOnline.com
http://runsmartonline.com/blog/mindfulness-improve-running-four-tips/

54. Meditation In Action: How To Turn Running Into A Mindfulness Practice - Headspace - HuffingtonPost.com
https://www.huffingtonpost.com/2013/07/22/meditation-in-action-running-mindfulness_n_3625110.html

55. Your Morning Cup of Tea or Coffee Can Be Your Meditation - Ora Nadrich - HuffingtonPost.com
https://www.huffingtonpost.com/ora-nadrich/meditation-practice_b_2114526.html

56. Get More from Your Glass of Wine with this Mindful Drinking Exercise - Elaine Smookler - Mindful.org https://www.mindful.org/get-more-from-your-glass-of-wine-with-this-mindful-drinking-exercise/

57. 6 Ways to Practice Mindful Eating - Christopher Willard - Mindful.org https://www.mindful.org/6-ways-practice-mindful-eating/

58. How to eat mindfully - Nancy Siragusa - BBCGoodFood.com https://www.bbcgoodfood.com/howto/guide/how-eat-mindfully

59. How the Brain Changes When You Meditate - Jennifer Wolkin - Mindful.org https://www.mindful.org/how-the-brain-changes-when-you-meditate/

60. How to Choose a Type of Mindfulness Meditation - Kira M. Newman - Mindful.org https://www.mindful.org/choose-type-mindfulness-meditation/

61. Calming an Anxious Mind - Release the Critic https://www.mindful.org/3-mindful-ways-calm-anxious-mind/

ABOUT THE AUTHOR

John Burley lives in Hertfordshire in the United Kingdom and at the point of writing this book runs a software development company producing software solutions to mainly the gaming industry. In recent months he has also been writing articles and a blog about the benefits of mindfulness, which has been receiving positive comments and feedback since it's launch.

www.johnburley.co.uk
www.mindfulnessforthemindless.com
www.amindfulway.blog

ACKNOWLEDGMENTS

A huge thank you to Megan, as without you this book would not have likely taken place. I will always be grateful to my phantom of delight.

A big thank you to Saber, Moushumi, Jenny, Bernadine, Dawn, Evelyn, Darren and Damian for your continued support and encouragement. An especially big thank you goes to Jenny and Saber for your immense and impressive efforts in the proof reading of this.

I also thank Craig and Saber for being the first of many to suggest that I actually sit down and write down all that I have learned about mindfulness, and to share it with the wider world instead of selfishly just with my friends and family. I hope the wider world now appreciates this :)

I thank Moushumi and Derek for both suggesting the original starting point for my journey of which Mindfulness became just one stop in the end. Who could have known then where it would all lead.

If I have missed anyone else, I am sorry, but thank you too. On my travels I have spoken with so many people, trying to explain mindfulness in the hope that it can help them improve their lives in some way. That it might help in working through their issues and help in solving their problems. Thanks for listening to me and I hope I did help in some way. Good luck to you all, and I really hope you find a path to a happier life, and that this book might help explain more than I ever could at the time.

I also thank all the people, many I will probably never meet again, for their views and opinions of the various cover designs. I think I got there in the end. Sorry if your choice didn't make it to print but all comments were heard and made a difference.

Finally, I thank Luke, Libby, Jenny, Thomas, Daniel, Katherine, William, Joseph, Dawn, Torran, Alba, Eva, Megan, Zachary and Abigail for their love and support through times, that all contributed to the journey into the wonderful future that I am charging towards. I am truly grateful and love you all very much.

25886729R00150

Printed in Poland
by Amazon Fulfillment
Poland Sp. z o.o., Wrocław